T0293968

WALKING ON LANZAROTE
AND FUERTEVENTURA

About the Author

Paddy Dillon is a prolific walker and guide-book writer, with over 60 books to his name and contributions to 25 other books. He has written for several outdoor magazines and other publications, and has appeared on radio and television.

Paddy has walked extensively around all the Canary Islands for this series of guides, along rugged cliff coasts, crossing deep and rocky *barrancos* and climbing all the highest mountains. He uses a tablet computer to write as he walks. This makes his descriptions, written at the very point at which the reader uses them, highly accurate and easy to follow on the ground.

Paddy is an indefatigable long-distance walker who has walked all of Britain's National Trails and several major European trails. He has also walked in Nepal, Tibet, and the Rocky Mountains of Canada and the US. Paddy is a member of the Outdoor Writers and Photographers Guild.

Other Cicerone guides by the author

GR20: Corsica
Irish Coastal Walks
The Cleveland Way and the
   Yorkshire Wolds Way
The GR5 Trail
The Great Glen Way
The Irish Coast to Coast Walk
The Mountains of Ireland
The National Trails
The North York Moors
The Pennine Way
The Reivers Way
The South West Coast Path
The Teesdale Way (Martin Collins;
   updated by Paddy Dillon)
Trekking in Greenland
Trekking in the Alps (contributing
   author)

Trekking through Mallorca
Walking and Trekking in Iceland
Walking in County Durham
Walking in Madeira
Walking in Mallorca (June Parker;
   updated by Paddy Dillon)
Walking in Malta
Walking in Sardinia
Walking in the Isles of Scilly
Walking in the North Pennines
Walking on Guernsey
Walking on Jersey
Walking on La Gomera and El
   Hierro
Walking on La Palma
Walking on Tenerife
Walking on the Isle of Arran
Walking the Galloway Hills

WALKING ON LANZAROTE AND FUERTEVENTURA

by Paddy Dillon

2 POLICE SQUARE, MILNTHORPE, CUMBRIA LA7 7PY
www.cicerone.co.uk

© Paddy Dillon 2014
First edition 2014
ISBN: 978 1 85284 603 9

Walking in the Canary Islands, Vol 1: West
ISBN: 978 1 85284 365 6
Walking in the Canary Islands, Vol 2: East
ISBN: 978 1 85284 368 7

Printed by KHL Printing, Singapore

A catalogue record for this book is available from the British Library.

All photographs are by the author unless otherwise stated.

Updates to this Guide

While every effort is made by our authors to ensure the accuracy of guidebooks as they go to print, changes can occur during the lifetime of an edition. If we know of any, there will be an Updates tab on this book's page on the Cicerone website (www.cicerone.co.uk), so please check before planning your trip. We also advise that you check information about such things as transport, accommodation and shops locally. Even rights of way can be altered over time. We are always grateful for information about any discrepancies between a guidebook and the facts on the ground, sent by email to info@cicerone.co.uk or by post to Cicerone, 2 Police Square, Milnthorpe LA7 7PY, United Kingdom.

Front cover: The gentle Barranco de Ajuy in Fuerteventura (Walk 29)

CONTENTS

Ancient, worn, volcanic hills rise in the middle of Isla La Graciosa

Map Key

	major roads
	walking route
····················	alternative route
-------------------	dirt track
·················	seasonal river
	river
	sea/reservoir
	town
▲	peak
■	habitation
●	viewpoint
•	fuente/spring
©	cave
=	bridge
→	route direction
→	direction arrow
Ⓢ Ⓕ	start point/finish point
ⓈⒻ	start/finish point
ⒶⓈ	alternative start point
ⒶⒻ	alternative finish point
ⒶⓈⒻ	alternative start/alternative finish point

Contour Key

	sea level		500–600m
	0–100m		600–700m
	100–200m		700–800m
	200–300m		
	300–400m		Map scale
	400–500m		

0 ———————————— 2km

0 ———————————— 1 mile

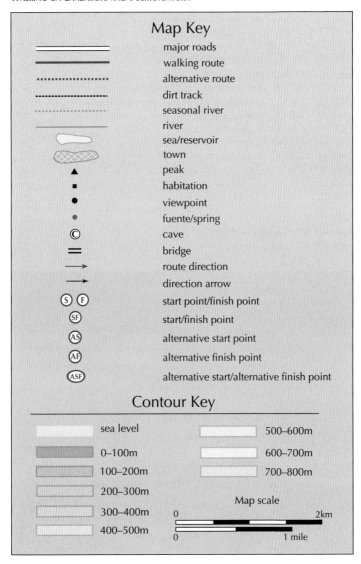

8

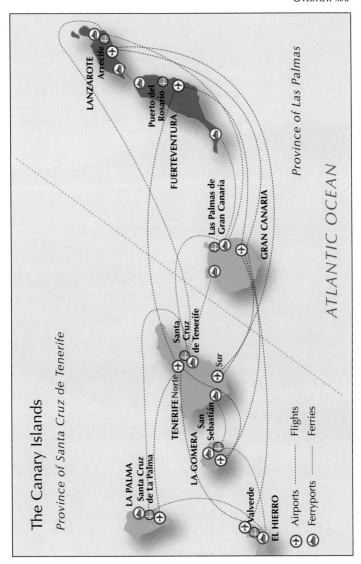

The Canary Islands
Province of Santa Cruz de Tenerife

Province of Las Palmas

ATLANTIC OCEAN

LANZAROTE
Arrecife

Puerto del
Rosario

FUERTEVENTURA

Las Palmas de
Gran Canaria

GRAN CANARIA

Santa
Cruz
de
Tenerife

Sur

TENERIFE Norte

San
Sebastián

LA GOMERA

LA PALMA
Santa Cruz
de La Palma

Valverde

EL HIERRO

Airports ─── Flights
Ferryports ┈┈┈ Ferries

Walkers crossing the barren Barranco de la Casita on Lanzarote, near a small shelter (Walk 1, Lanzarote)

INTRODUCTION

Walkers leaving the summit of Morro de la Loma del Pozo, heading for the Barranco de la Higuera (Walk 1, Lanzarote)

The seven sub-tropical Canary Islands bask in sunny splendour off the Atlantic coast of north-west Africa. Millions of sun-starved north Europeans flock there for beach holidays, but increasingly visitors are discovering the amazing variety of landscapes throughout the archipelago. Conditions range from semi-deserts to perpetually moist *laurisilva* 'cloud forests', from rugged cliff coasts to high mountains, from fertile cultivation terraces to awesome rocky *barrancos* carved deep into multi-coloured layers of volcanic bedrock. Some areas are given the highest possible protection as national parks, but there are many more types of protected landscapes, rural parks, natural monuments and nature reserves.

More and more walkers are finding their feet, exploring the Canary Islands using centuries-old mule tracks, rugged cliff paths and forest trails. Paths pick their way between cultivation terraces, squeeze between houses and make their way to rugged coves and hidden beaches. Some paths run from village to village, following old mule tracks once used to transport goods, while other paths are based on pilgrim trails to and from remote churches and *ermitas*. Many have been cleared, repaired, signposted and waymarked in recent years, ready to be explored and enjoyed.

This guidebook explores the waymarked trail networks on the large islands of Lanzarote and Fuerteventura. They include routes of all types, from easy strolls to steep and rugged slopes; from simple day walks to long-distance trails. As these routes are often fully signposted and waymarked, walkers can follow them with confidence and enjoy the islands to the full. Around 710km (440 miles) of trails are described in this guidebook.

LOCATION

The Canary Islands are more or less enclosed in a rectangular area from 13°30'W to 18°00'W and 27°30'N to 29°30'N. As a group, they stretch west to east over 450km (280 miles). Although administered by Spain, the mother country is 1100km (685 miles) away. The narrowest strait between the Canary Islands and Africa is a mere 110km (70 miles). The total land area is almost 7500km (2900 square miles), but the sea they occupy is 10 times that size.

GEOLOGY

Most of the world's volcanic landscapes are formed where huge continental or oceanic 'plates' collide with each other. When continental plates collide, the Earth's crust crumples upwards to form mountains, and when plates are torn apart, basaltic rock from deep within the Earth's mantle erupts to form mountains. The

La Geria on Lanzarote, where ash pits and semi-circular walls protect vines from the wind

Canary Islands, however, are different, and have a complicated geological history.

The African landmass is the visible part of a continental plate that extends into the Atlantic Ocean, but the Canary Islands lie within the oceanic crust of the eastern Atlantic Ocean, close to the passive junction with the African continental plate. It is thought that the islands now lie directly above a hot-spot, or mantle plume, some 2500km (1550 miles) deep within the Earth. The mantle plume is fixed, but the oceanic and African plates are drifting very slowly eastwards. Every so often a split in the oceanic crust opens above the mantle plume, allowing molten rock to vent onto the ocean floor. As more and more material erupts, it piles higher and higher until it rises from the sea. Each of the Canary Islands was formed this way.

Lanzarote and Fuerteventura were the first Canary Islands to form, and were subsequently pulled eastwards. The next time a rift opened, the islands of Gran Canaria and Tenerife were formed, and these were in turn pulled eastwards. A further oceanic rift led to the formation of La Gomera, La Palma and El Hierro. Looking forward in geological time more islands will appear as the rift is torn open in the future.

The forces at work deep within the Earth can scarcely be imagined. Every single piece of rock throughout the Canary Islands once existed in a

Many recent lava flows display a 'ropey' surface, showing exactly how the molten rock solidified

molten state. Consider the energy needed to melt one small stone, and multiply that to imagine the energy required to melt everything in the island chain, as well as the immense amount of rock beneath the sea that supports them all!

Over time huge amounts of volcanic material were piled high, but erosion has led to great instability. During recent geological time, vast chunks of the islands collapsed into the sea, creating features such as El Golfo on El Hierro, the Caldera de Taburiente on La Palma, and the Orotava valley on Tenerife. With each catastrophic collapse, tidal waves devastated places around the Atlantic Ocean. Some geologists believe that the steep, bulging northern slope of El Teide could collapse during any future volcanic eruption.

WILDLIFE

Plants and flowers

While the northern hemisphere was in the grip of an Ice Age, the Canary Islands were sluiced by rainstorms, with powerful rivers carving deep, steep-sided barrancos into unstable layers of ash and lava. As the land-masses emerged from the Ice Age, the Canary Islands dried out and the vegetation had to adapt to survive. Some species are well adapted to semi-desert conditions, while on the highest parts of the islands, laurisilva 'cloud forests' are able to trap moisture from the mists and keep themselves well watered. Laurisilva forests once spread all the way round the Mediterranean and tropical regions. Small remnants of this forest survive on the higher northern slopes of most of the Canary Islands, but not on Lanzarote or Fuerteventura.

(top to bottom) The squat and spiky cardón de Jandía is endemic to the Jandía peninsula on Fuerteventura; uvilla, looking like a little bunch of grapes, is found along arid coastlines; rubbery-stalked verode is a common sight in scrub on all the islands

Canary pines flourish on high, dry mountainsides, sometimes in places where nothing else grows. However, these are very rare on Lanzarote and Fuerteventura, where most of the trees are Canary palms. These flourish in dry places, and in the past every part of the tree had a use; today they provide delicious *miel de palma*, or palm syrup. Every so often you might come across a dragon tree, the last surviving descendants of ancient prehistoric forests. They have been decimated in the wild but prove popular in gardens.

Tagasaste trees are found in dense plantations on the western islands, but not on Lanzarote and Fuerteventura. They grow with little water, yet have a high nutritional content and are regularly cut for animal fodder. In recent years they have been exported to Australia. Fruit and nut trees have been established, including oranges, lemons, almonds, figs and vines, but Lanzarote and Fuerteventura are not ideal for growing bananas. Introduced prickly pears are abundant, not so much for their fruit, but for raising cochineal beetles, whose blood provides a vivid red dye.

Bushy scrub is rich and varied, including a host of species that walkers will become familiar with. These include bushy, rubbery *tabaibal* and tall *cardón*, or candelabra spurge. Both have milky latex sap, as does *aulaga*, which looks like a tangled mass of spines and is often found colonising old cultivation terraces in arid areas. Along the coast succulent plants thrive, such as *uvilla*, which looks like bunches of tiny grapes. The fragrant Canarian lavender usually grows in arid, rocky, stony areas among other scrub species. Of particular importance on Fuerteventura is the *cardón de Jandía*, which grows only on the Jandía peninsula. Few of the plants have common English names, but all of them feature so often that they should be learned.

Flowers grow all year round, but visitors in spring and early summer will be amazed at the colour and wealth of flowering plants. Many are Canarian endemics, and even trying to compile a shortlist would be pointless. Anyone with a particular interest in flowers and other plants should carry a specific field guide, in English. Try *Native Flora of the Canary Islands* by Miguel Ángel Cabrera Pérez (Editorial Everest) or *Wild Flowers of the Canary Islands* by David Bramwell and Zoë Bramwell (Editorial Rueda).

Animals
As befits remote islands created in relatively recent geological time, the main animal groups to colonise the land were winged creatures, insects and birds. The largest indigenous land mammals were bats. Large and small lizards also arrived, possibly clinging to driftwood.

The laurisilva cloud forest is home to the laurel pigeon, while the rock pigeon prefers cliffs. Buzzards and kestrels can be spotted hunting, and ospreys are making a slow comeback.

Waves pound against low cliffs around the Playa de Ojos (Walk 24, Jandía)

Ravens and choughs are common in some places. There are several varieties of pipits, chaffinches, warblers and chiffchaffs. One of the smallest birds is the kinglet, a relative of the goldcrest. There are canaries, which have nothing to do with the name of the islands, and hoopoes can also be spotted. The islands attract plenty of passage migrants, as well as escapees from aviaries. The coastal fringes are colonised by gulls, but it is best to take a boat trip to spot shearwaters or storm petrels, as they spend most of their time on open water. Boat trips are also the way to spot a variety of dolphins and whales.

Once the Guanche people arrived and colonised the islands over 2000 years ago, the forests suffered as much from clearance as from grazing by voracious sheep and goats.

Following the Conquest in the 15th century, the Spanish brought in other domestic animals; of these the cats had a particularly devastating impact on the native wildlife, practically wiping out giant Canarian lizards, which have only recently been rescued from the edge of extinction on El

Ground squirrels can now be found on Fuerteventura but are not native to the Canaries

Hierro. The lizards seen on Lanzarote and Fuerteventura are much smaller. Rabbits chew their way through the vegetation and appear regularly on Canarian menus. Ground squirrels are often seen on Fuerteventura, but aren't found on the other islands.

NATIONAL PARKS

The Canary Islands include a handful of national parks and many other protected areas. There is no national park on Fuerteventura, but large parts of the island have been protected in other ways, such as Parque Rural (Rural Park), Parque Natural (Natural Park), Paisaje Protegido (Protected Land), Reserva Natural Especial (Special Nature Reserve), Monumento Natural (Natural Monument), and so on. Lanzarote has the Parque Nacional

de Timanfaya, which is so strictly controlled that it is a forbidden to set foot on it! Prominent notices usually tell walkers when they are entering or leaving protected areas. There are visitor centres where more information can be studied, and where interesting literature is on sale.

THE FORTUNATE ISLES

Myths and legends speak of 'The Fortunate Isles', or 'Isles of the Blessed', lying somewhere in the Atlantic, enjoying a wonderful climate and bearing all manner of fruit. The rebel Roman general Sertorius planned to retire there, while Plutarch referred to them many times. Pliny, though, warned 'these islands, however, are greatly annoyed by the putrefying bodies of monsters, which

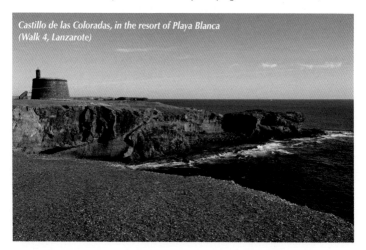

Castillo de las Coloradas, in the resort of Playa Blanca
(Walk 4, Lanzarote)

The remarkable landmark of Torrecilla, and the jagged crater rim of Monte Corona (Walk 23, Lanzarote)

are constantly thrown up by the sea.' Maybe these scribes knew of the Canary Islands, or maybe they were drawing on older Phoenician or Carthaginian references. Some would even claim that the islands were the last remnants of Atlantis.

The Gaunches, often described as a 'stone age' civilisation, settled on the Canary Islands well over 2000 years ago, and Cro-Magnon man was there as early as 3000BC. No-one knows where the Guanches came from, but it seems likely they arrived from North Africa in fleets of canoes. Although technologically primitive, their society was well-ordered, and they had a special regard for monumental rock-forms in the mountains.

The Guanches fiercely resisted the well-armed Spaniards during the 14th century Conquest of the islands,

but one by one each island fell. Tenerife capitulated last of all, with the mighty volcano of El Teide grumbling throughout. Many Guanches were slaughtered or enslaved, but some entered into treaties, converted to Christianity and inter-married. They lost their land and freedom, but their blood flows in the veins of native Canarios.

The Canary Islands were visited by Christopher Columbus on his voyage of discovery in 1492. Subsequently they were used as stepping-stones to the Americas, with many Canarios emigrating. The islands were exposed and not always defended with military might; they were subject to pirate raids, endured disputes with the Portuguese, were attacked by the British and suffered wavering economic fortunes.

There was constant rivalry between Tenerife and Gran Canaria, with the entire island group being governed from Las Palmas de Gran Canaria from 1808, before Santa Cruz de Tenerife became the capital in 1822. In 1927 the Canary Islands were divided into two provinces – Las Palmas and Santa Cruz de Tenerife.

In the early 20th century the military governor of the islands, General Franco, launched a military coup from Tenerife. This led to the creation of the Spanish Republic, marking the onset of the infamous Civil War and a long dictatorship. The islands remained free of the worst strife of the Civil War, but also became something of a backwater; it was largely as a result of Franco's later policies that they were developed from the 1960s as a major destination for northern Europeans.

Since 1982 the islands have been an autonomous region and there have been calls for complete independence from Spain. The islanders regard themselves as 'Canarios' first and 'Spanish' second, although they are also fiercely loyal to their own particular islands, towns and villages.

GETTING THERE

There are plenty of options for flying direct to Lanzarote and Fuerteventura, scheduled and charter, from many British and European airports. The hardest part is checking all the 'deals' to find an airport, operator, schedules and prices that suit. Both international

and domestic flights operate from the airports on both islands.

Frequent, fast and cheap buses link the airports with the main towns and resorts, and the taxi fares are reasonable. Two ferry companies offer rapid and regular services between Lanzarote and Fuerteventura – Lineas Fred Olsen and Naviera Armas.

WHEN TO GO

Most people visit the Canary Islands in summer, but it is usually too hot for walking. Winter weather is often good, but on Lanzarote and Fuerteventura expect some cloud cover and a little rain at times, as well as near-constant strong winds. Spring weather is sunny and clear, while the vegetation is fresh and features an amazing wealth of flowers. Autumn weather is often good, but the vegetation often seems rather scorched after the summer.

ACCOMMODATION

Most visitors to the Canary Islands opt for a package deal, so they are tied to a single accommodation base in a faceless resort. This is far from ideal and a base in the 'wrong' place can make it difficult to get to and from walking routes. Out of season, walkers would have no problem turning up unannounced on the doorsteps of hotels and pensións and securing accommodation. It's also possible to take short self-catering lets with ease

Wild camping is illegal, but a few campsites are available to permit-holders

– simply check accommodation websites for leads and to make bookings.

Opportunities to camp are limited, and while campsites are entirely free of charge, permits have to be applied for in advance and collected in person before travelling to a campsite. Wild camping is technically illegal but surprisingly popular.

The contact details of all the local tourist information offices are given in the part introductions and in Appendix C.

HEALTH AND SAFETY

There are no nasty diseases on the Canary Islands, or at least nothing you couldn't contract at home. Water on Lanzarote and Fuerteventura is mostly from desalination plants, with some rainfall impounded in reservoirs. Either way, it is clean and safe to drink, although some people don't like the taste. Bottled water is available if you prefer, but buy it cheaply from supermarkets rather than at considerable expense from bars. There are no snakes and no stinging insects worse than honey-bees. Don't annoy dogs and they won't annoy you. Dogs that are likely to bite are nearly always tethered, so keep away.

In case of a medical emergency, dial 112 for an ambulance. In case of a non-emergency, all islands have hospitals, health centres (*Centro de Salud*) and chemists (*Farmacia*). If treatment is required, EU citizens should present their European Health Insurance Card, which may help to offset some costs.

FOOD AND DRINK

Every town and most of the villages throughout the Canary Islands have bars. Most bars also double as cafés or restaurants, often serving tapas, which are often in glass cabinets, so you can point to the ones you want to eat. Shops are often available, selling local and imported foodstuffs. Always make the effort to sample local fare, which can be interesting and very tasty. The availability of refreshments is mentioned on every walking trail, but bear in mind that opening hours are

Cooking on top of a volcanic vent at the restaurant in the Parque Nacional de Timanfaya on Lanzarote

variable. Some shops take a very long lunch break, and not all businesses are open every day of the week. Some shops are closed all weekend, or at least half of Saturday and all of Sunday.

LANGUAGE

Castilian Spanish is spoken throughout the Canary Islands, although in most resorts and large hotels there are English and German speakers. Those who travel to remote rural parts will need at least a few basic phrases of Spanish. Anyone with any proficiency in Spanish will quickly realise that the Canarios have their own accent and colloquialisms; for instance, the letter 's' often vanishes from the middle or end of words, to be replaced by a gentle 'h', or even a completely

soundless gap. Listen very carefully to distinguish between '*La Palma*' (the island) and '*Las Palmas*' (the city). The latter becomes '*Lah Palmah*'. A bus is referred to as an *autobus* in Spain, but as a *guagua* throughout the Canary Islands. Some natives may sieze the opportunity to practice their English with you, while others may be puzzled by your accent. No matter how bad you think you sound, you will not be the worst they've heard!

A basic glossary of useful topographical words for walkers is provided in Appendix B.

MONEY

The Euro is the currency of the Canary Islands. Large denomination Euro notes are difficult to use for small purchases, so avoid the €500 and €200 notes altogether, and avoid the €100 notes if you can. The rest are fine: €50, €20, €10 and €5. Coins come in €2 and €1. Small denomination coins come in values of 50c, 20c, 10c, 5c, 2c and 1c. Banks and ATMs are mentioned where they occur, if cash is needed. Many accommodation providers accept major credit and debit cards, as will large supermarkets, but small bars, shops and cafés deal only in cash.

COMMUNICATIONS

All the towns and some of the villages have post offices (*Correos*) and public telephones. Opening times for large post offices are usually 0830–1430 Monday to Friday, 0930–1300 Saturday, closed on Sunday. Small post offices have more limited opening times. Mobile phone coverage is usually good in towns and villages, but can be completely absent elsewhere, depending on the nature of the terrain. High mountains and deep barrancos block signals. Internet access is sometimes offered by hotels; if relying on it, please check while making a booking.

WALKING ON LANZAROTE AND FUERTEVENTURA

Lanzarote and Fuerteventura are the two easternmost Canary Islands, closest to the west coast of Africa and the Sahara Desert. Rather oddly, these two islands lie closer together than any of the other islands, but at the same time lie further from their neighbours than any of the other islands. They also lie lower than the more mountainous

Looking down the path from Montaña de Cardón to Montaña Redondo (Walk 28, Fuerteventura)

22

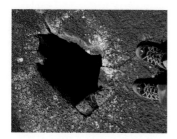

Walking off-trail on lava flows is not recommended, as thin rock crusts may conceal deep holes

islands further west, and as a result have less rainfall, making them appear particularly arid in many places and even quite desert-like at times. With little shade, walkers need to protect themselves from the sun as much as possible. These islands are often windier than their western counterparts, and occasionally lie in the path of dust storms from the Sahara Desert.

Despite the scarcity of water on Lanzarote and Fuerteventura, agriculture is important. Extensive areas have been farmed in the past, but many of these parts have been abandoned, with efforts concentrated elsewhere. Most walkers prefer the hillier regions with their extensive views, rather than the lowlands, and most of the walks in this book enjoy some measure of elevation. In recent years many of the old paths in the hills, often linking villages together, have been cleared, restored, signposted and waymarked. Also, a long distance trail, designated as the GR 131, stretches along the length of both islands, as well as crossing other islands further west. Walks on Lanzarote are described in the first half of this book, with walks on Fuerteventura described in the second half.

WHAT TO TAKE

If planning to use one or two bases to explore, then a simple day pack is all you need, containing items you would normally take for a day walk. Waterproofs can be lightweight and might not even be used. Footwear is a personal preference, but wear what you would normally wear for rocky, stony slopes, remembering that hot feet are more likely to be a problem than wet feet. Lightweight, light-coloured clothing is best in bright sunshine, along with a sun hat and frequent applications of sunscreen.

If planning to backpack around the islands, bear in mind that there are some very basic camp-grounds but permits have to be negotiated in order to use them. This can be confusing and time-consuming for a visitor, as it requires negotiations with municipal authorities and collection of paperwork. Wild camping is technically illegal but surprisingly popular. Lightweight kit should be carried, as a heavy pack is a cruel burden in hot weather. Water can be difficult to find, so try and anticipate your needs and carry enough to last until you reach a village, houses or bar where you can obtain a refill.

WAYMARKING AND ACCESS

Lanzarote and Fuerteventura only recently adopted a system for signposting and waymarking routes using standard European codes. The islands have networks of short PR (*pequeño recorrido*) routes, which are marked with yellow and white paint flashes, and numbered to keep them separate. Signposts will read 'PR LZ...' or 'PR FV...' with a number following the letters. These codes are quoted in the route descriptions so that walkers will always be able to check they are going the right way. There are also GR (*gran recorrido*) routes traversing both islands; these are intended as long-distance walks but can also serve as simple one-day linear walks. Some short links are marked as SL (*sendero local* – literally 'local walk').

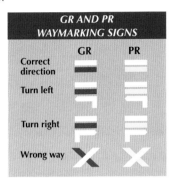

GR AND PR WAYMARKING SIGNS

	GR	PR
Correct direction		
Turn left		
Turn right		
Wrong way		

Apart from signposts, routes are marked by occasional paint marks, parallel yellow and white stripes for the PR routes, with red and white stripes for the GR routes and green and white stripes for the SL routes. These confirm that walkers are still on course, and usually appear at

A sandy track runs along a broad crest across the desert-like expanse of El Jable (Walk 39, Fuerteventura)

junctions. Left and right turns are indicated with right-angled flashes, but if the paint marks form an 'X', this indicates that a wrong turn has been made.

MAPS

The Instituto Geográfico Nacional (IGN), www.cnig.es, publishes maps of the Canary Islands at scales of 1:50,000 and 1:25,000. These are part of the Mapa Topográfico Nacional (MTN) series. To avoid disappointment, please check the style and quality of these maps before making a purchase, since they generally don't show the sort of details that walkers require.

The best general maps of Lanzarote and Fuerteventura are the 1:50,000 Kompass maps, available in Britain with an Automobile Association cover as AA Island Series 6 – Fuerteventura, and AA Island Series 9 – Lanzarote. The evolving trail network does not yet fully feature on maps, although routes are often outlined on map-boards around the islands, from which details can be copied and transferred to other maps.

Maps can be ordered in advance from British suppliers such as: Stanfords (12–14 Long Acre, London, WC2E 9LP, tel. 020 7836 1321, www.stanfords.co.uk), The Map Shop (15 High Street, Upton-upon-Severn, WR8 0HJ, tel. 01684 593146, www.themapshop.co.uk) or Cordee (tel. 01455 611185, www.cordee.co.uk).

The sketch maps in this guidebook are at a scale of 1:50,000. Routes marked on them can be transferred to other maps if required.

EMERGENCIES

The pan-European emergency telephone number 112 is used to call for assistance throughout the Canary Islands, linking with the police, fire or ambulance service, for a response on land or at sea. The Guardia Civil telephone number is 062, and it is likely they would be involved in a response involving mountain rescue, as they generally patrol rural areas.

USING THIS GUIDE

The walks are spread around the islands, and where they lie side-by-side, links between routes are often possible. Day walks are described around Lanzarote, exploring hill, coast and village-to-village trails, generally working from south to north, ending on the small island of La Graciosa. The long-distance GR 131 is then followed from south to north through the island. More day walks are described on Fuerteventura, again working from south to north, followed by another, longer stretch of the GR 131 through the island, ending on the little island of Lobos.

A summary table of all the key information about the routes described in this guide is provided as Appendix A.

Evening light near Montaña de la Fuente, looking towards the villages of Pájara and Toto (Walk 40, Fuerteventura)

On arrival on Lanzarote and Fuerteventura, visit a tourist information office (see Appendix C) as soon as possible and ask for an accommodation list along with any information about walking opportunities that they stock. Remember to pick up leaflets about any visitor attractions that seem interesting, as they usually give full contact details, opening times and admission charges. For up-to-date bus timetables go to intercitybuslanzarote. es (Lanzarote) and www.maxorata bus.com (Fuerteventura). After that, you should have all the information you need to enjoy the walks to the maximum.

LANZAROTE

A rocky, sand-blown coastline finally leads to the surfing village of Caleta de Famara (Walk 11)

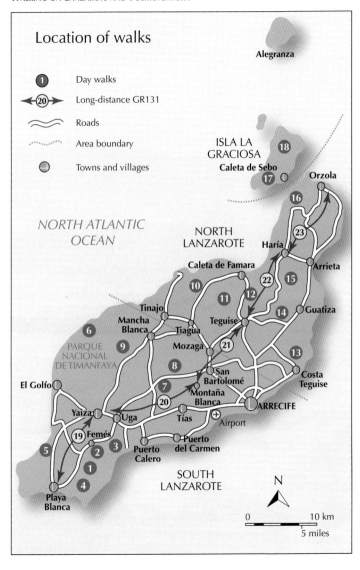

Location of walks

1 Day walks

◀**20**▶ Long-distance GR131

〰 Roads

······· Area boundary

◐ Towns and villages

Alegranza

ISLA LA GRACIOSA

18

17 Caleta de Sebo

Orzola

16

23

NORTH ATLANTIC OCEAN

NORTH LANZAROTE

Haría

Arrieta

Caleta de Famara

10

11

12

22

15

Tinajo

9

Mancha Blanca

Tiagua

14

Guatiza

Mozaga

Teguise

PARQUE NACIONAL DE TIMANFAYA

6

8

21

13

7

San Bartolomé

Costa Teguise

El Golfo

Montaña Blanca

20

Yaiza

Uga

Tías

ARRECIFE

Airport

19 Femés

2 **3**

Puerto Calero

Puerto del Carmen

5

1

SOUTH LANZAROTE

N

4

Playa Blanca

0   10 km

5 miles

INTRODUCTION

Hacha Chica, rising above barren, stony slopes near Papagayo, on the lower parts of Walk 4

Lanzarote is the fourth largest Canary Island, and while many of its areas are under cultivation, or swathed in rugged lava, there is plenty of scope for interesting and varied walks. Three weeks of walking are covered on Lanzarote, with another two days on the island of La Graciosa. The main town, Arrecife, is flanked by three resorts on the east coast, while there are only a couple of villages on the rugged west coast. The former capital, Teguise, lies in the centre of the island – a safe location when piracy was rife.

The day walks on the island may be circular or linear, and either way there are good bus services for joining and leaving routes. The long-distance GR 131, from Playa Blanca to Orzola, is very well served by buses. The Parque Nacional de Timanfaya has very limited access for walkers: a rugged coastal path, Walk 6, is available any time, but it is long and difficult, while the short Ruta de Termesana is only available by advance booking through the national park visitor centre. (See www.reservasparquesnacionales.es and select 'Timanfaya'.) Other guided walks are also available.

There are about 355km (220 miles) of walking on Lanzarote described in this book.

Looking from Fuerteventura to Lanzarote – barely half an hour's ferry journey connects them

GETTING THERE

By Air
Flights to Lanzarote from Gran Canaria and Tenerife are operated by Binter Canarias, tel. 902-391392, www. bintercanarias.com, and Canaryfly, tel. 902-808065, www.canaryfly.es. Buses meet incoming flights, offering links with Arrecife and the three resorts of Costa Teguise, Puerto del Carmen and Playa Blanca. Taxis are also available at the airport.

By Ferry
Two ferry companies operate regular services between Playa Blanca on Lanzarote and Corralejo on Fuerteventura: Lineas Fred Olsen, tel. 902-100107, www.fredolsen.es; and Naviera Armas, tel. 902-456500, www. naviera-armas.com. Less regular ferries link Arrecife with Las Palmas on Gran Canaria and Santa Cruz on Tenerife.

GETTING AROUND

By Bus
Lanzarote has a good network of bus services operated by IntercityBus, tel. 928-811522. The website, intercity buslanzarote.es, contains full timetable details and route maps. The bus station does not supply printed timetables! Tickets are for single journeys

and fares are paid on boarding the bus. Alternatively, buy a 'bono' card, load it with funds and enjoy a ten per cent discount on fares. Buses are referred to as *guaguas*, although bus stops, or *paradas*, may be marked as 'bus'. All the towns and most villages have bus services, while the Sunday market at Teguise has special services.

By Taxi

Long taxi rides are expensive, but short journeys are worth considering. The following numbers link with taxis around the island: Arrecife tel. 928-800806; Airport, Playa Honda and San Bartolomé tel. 928-520176; Playa Blanca and Yaiza tel. 928-524222; Puerto del Carmen and Tías tel. 928-524220; Tinajo and La Santa tel. 928-840049; Teguise and Costa Teguise tel. 928-524223; Haría and Orzola tel. 620-315350. Fares are fixed by the municipalities and can be inspected on demand, although negotiation might be possible.

ACCOMMODATION

Accommodation is abundant on Lanzarote, although it is concentrated in the resorts of Playa Blanca, Puerto del Carmen and Costa Teguise, as well as the capital Arrecife. Elsewhere, small hotels and rural properties are widely spread. Many places that were once reserved for package tourists now cheerfully offer rooms and services to people who book at short notice or via the internet.

FOOD AND DRINK

Lanzarote produces much of its own fruit, vegetables and fish. Some restaurants are cosmopolitan, while others offer good local fare. Specialities include goats' cheese. Wrinkly potatoes (*papas arrugadas*) cooked in salt are surprisingly refreshing in hot weather, served with hot *mojo roja* sauce or the gentler *mojo verde*. The fish used in most local fish dishes is *vieja*. If any dishes such as soups or stews need thickening, reach for the roasted flour *gofio*, which doubles as a breakfast cereal. Lanzarote also produces an abundance of wine. Never pass up an opportunity to indulge in local fare!

TOURIST INFORMATION OFFICES

Arrecife tel. 928-813174
Ferryport tel. 928-844690
Airport tel. 928-820704
Playa Blanca tel. 928-518150
San Bartolomé tel. 928-522351
Puerto del Carmen tel. 928-513351
Costa Teguise tel. 928-592542

The main tourism website for Lanzarote is www.turismolanzarote.com.

SOUTH LANZAROTE

The Ruta de Termesana in the Parque Nacional de Timanfaya is only available to pre-booked walkers

Most visitors stay in the southern half of Lanzarote, between Arrecife and Playa Blanca. Large areas of this region are protected, including the striking arid mountains of the Monumento Natural Los Ajaches.

The inter-linked Walks 1 to 4 explore the area, including parts of the coastline between Puerto Calero and Playa Blanca. More of the coast is explored on Walks 5 and 6, from Playa Blanca to Tinajo. Access to the Parque Nacional de Timanfaya is restricted, and the popular, short, guided Ruta de Termesana has to be booked through the national park visitor centre. (See www.reservasparquesnacionales.es, and choose 'Timanfaya'.)

Walk 7 runs from village to village through the Paisaje Protegido de La Geria, which is a notable wine-growing region covered in black volcanic ash. Walk 8 offers further access to the area, but also visits the Monumento Natural Cueva de los Naturalistas among awesome lava flows. Walk 9 wanders through the interesting Parque Natural de los Volcanes, where old volcanic cones stand as islands in extensive, rugged lava flows dating only from the 1730s. Note that it is easy to visit neighbouring Fuerteventura by ferry from Playa Blanca.

WALK 1

Femés and Barranco de la Casita

Start/Finish	Roundabout, Femés
Distance	8km (5 miles)
Total Ascent/Descent	430m (1410ft)
Time	2hrs 30min
Terrain	Mostly clear paths, but often on steep, stony and rocky slopes. Some stretches are unsuitable for vertigo sufferers.
Refreshment	Bar restaurants at Femés.
Transport	Occasional buses serve Femés on weekdays from Arrecife, Playa Honda and Tías.

This short, popular circular walk is also rough and stony, crossing steep, rocky slopes. Most walkers find it spectacular, but some might be unnerved by the exposure and steepness. The route cuts across rocky slopes, traversing barren barrancos where there are no signs of habitation, before returning to Femés.

▶ The last bus stop at **Femés** is near a little *supermercado*. There is a nearby roundabout with a palm tree at its centre and this is where the walk starts, around 370m (1215ft). First, take a look around the village – especially

Route uses PR LZ 09.

The village of Femés sits on a gap at the foot of Atalaya de Femés

33

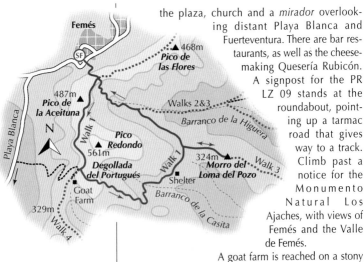

the plaza, church and a *mirador* overlooking distant Playa Blanca and Fuerteventura. There are bar restaurants, as well as the cheese-making Quesería Rubicón.

A signpost for the PR LZ 09 stands at the roundabout, pointing up a tarmac road that gives way to a track. Climb past a notice for the Monumento Natural Los Ajaches, with views of Femés and the Valle de Femés.

A goat farm is reached on a stony gap at Loma Pico de la Aceituna, at 414m (1358ft). Two mapboards and two signposts stand to the right. The PR LZ 09 heads right, and is easy to spot as it has a black plastic water pipe alongside. ◄ The path crosses the steep and rocky **Pico de la Aceituna**, and while it is technically easy to walk, you cannot afford to trip or stumble. The rock comes in pastel shades, exposed to the elements by serious over-grazing. The view down the **Barranco de la Higuera** extends along the coast to built-up resorts and distant Arrecife. Despite the steepness of the slope, the path runs gently down and up, squeezing past prickly pears at one point.

Rise and cross a stony gap at 441m (1447ft), then follow the path round the steep, rocky slopes of **Pico Redondo**. The water pipe still runs alongside, and views stretch towards Playa Blanca and Fuerteventura. There are more prickly pears but otherwise the mountainside is bare and over-grazed. When a fork is reached above **Degollada del Portugués**, keep left and follow the path uphill, crossing a broad and stony shoulder around 440m (1445ft). ◄ The views are lost as the path zigzags

The PR LZ 10-11 heads left, followed on Walk 2 and Walk 3.

The path descending to the right is used on Walk 4.

34

downhill. The ground is entirely stony, dotted with a few tabaibal. Walk along a crest to a tumbled drystone enclosure and a marker post. Turn left and zigzag down into the **Barranco de la Casita**, passing a few prickly pears and crossing the bed around 240m (790ft).

The path climbs quickly to a little **shelter** beside an old rainwater collector, where a left turn leads gently up to a broad gap covered in bright stones, where there are also old marker posts, at 285m (935ft). At this point, it is well worth turning right to follow a path, or a track running parallel, along a gentle, stony crest dotted with tabaibal. The summit of **Morro de la Loma del Pozo** is crowned with a cairn and prickly pears at 324m (1063ft). ▶ Enjoy fine views of Los Ajaches, with Arrecife, Lobos and Fuerteventura in the distance. Double back to the broad gap of bright stones and be sure to follow a path, not a track, down into the **Barranco de la Higuera**. The path runs gradually down across a rugged slope, then rises towards a pylon where a right turn leads down to a three-way signpost at around 260m (855ft). ▶

Turn left and follow a path towards the rock-walled head of the barranco. Swing right; the path is crudely paved in places, gradually rising across a steep and rocky slope. Stones and boulders are scattered everywhere, but the way ahead is obvious, exploiting soft beds of rock and eventually returning to the goat farm at Loma Pico de la Aceituna. Simply walk down the access track and road to return to **Femés**.

It is possible to continue along the crest, descending towards the coast, to link with coastal paths.

Walk 2 is joined here.

WALK 2

Femés and Pico de las Flores

Start/Finish	Roundabout, Femés
Distance	10km (6¼ miles)
Total Ascent/Descent	420m (1380ft)
Time	3hrs
Terrain	Mostly clear paths, initially stony and rocky underfoot, on steep, stony and rocky slopes, with a vague stretch later.
Refreshment	Bar restaurants at Femés
Transport	Occasional buses serve Femés on weekdays from Arrecife, Playa Honda and Tías.

This short, circular walk takes in the Barranco de la Higuera and rugged little mountains alongside the Valle de Femés, between Las Casitas and Femés. Apart from a rugged descent soon after starting, most of the other paths are fairly easy and offer splendid views around the mountain range of Los Ajaches.

Route uses PR LZ 10, 11 and 12.

◀ The last bus stop at **Femés** is near a little supermercado. There is a nearby roundabout with a palm tree at its centre and this is where the walk starts, around 370m (1215ft). First, take a look around the village – especially the plaza, church and a mirador overlooking distant Playa Blanca and Fuerteventura. There are bar restaurants, as well as the cheese-making Quesería Rubicón. A signpost for the PR LZ 09 stands at the roundabout, pointing up a tarmac road that gives way to a track. Climb past a notice for the Monumento Natural Los Ajaches, with views of Femés and the Valle de Femés.

A goat farm is reached on a stony gap at Loma Pico de la Aceituna, at 414m (1358ft). Two mapboards and two signposts stand to the right. The PR LZ 10-11 heads left, but almost immediately turns right. ◀ A broad path, covered in stones and boulders, drops steeply across a

The PR LZ 09 heads right, followed on Walk 1 and Walk 4.

The path climbing from the Valle del Pozo to the gap of Loma Pico de Naos

rocky slope while exploiting soft beds of rock. There is crude stone paving later, then the path swings left and runs down to a three-way signpost in the **Barranco de la Higuera**, around 260m (855ft). ▶ Keep left, or straight ahead through the barranco, roughly following pylons to reach another signpost at 127m (417ft).

Take careful note of where the signpost actually points. Most walkers continue to the coast, which is covered in Walk 3, but our route follows a vague path running parallel to the track, just to the left,

Walk 1 joins from the right.

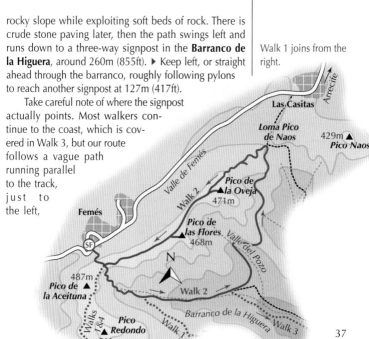

37

becoming clearer only as it drifts away from the track. This is the PR LZ 10-12 for Loma Pico de Naos. The path rises gently into **Valle del Pozo**, following a dry streambed for a while. Exit on the right past prickly pears and follow the path across a crest around 220m (720ft). The path is unmistakeable, looping in and out of gullies on the mountainside, passing more prickly pears and becoming rockier as it rises. Reach a track on a gap at **Loma Pico de Naos**, at 302m (991ft), where there is a turning space. ◄

The track leads, in less than 1km (½ mile) to bus stops at Las Casitas.

A path on the left climbs south-west, later zigzagging uphill. It then has rock rising to the left, and tabaibal dotted around, before reaching a bare gap. At this point it is worth turning sharp left up a short path to a rocky little summit at 375m (1230ft) bearing prickly pears. The path continues from the bare gap, zigzagging uphill and reaching a fork. Keep left along the higher path, but if the other is taken in error, both paths rejoin later. It is again worth making a sharp left turn to climb to the summit of **Pico de la Oveja**, at 471m (1545ft), to enjoy fine views. On the way to the gap beyond, the slopes become bouldery and the path is more rugged. Either pass or climb **Pico de las Flores**, then continue towards buildings on the next gap. This is the goat farm on Loma Pico de la Aceituna, passed earlier in the day. Simply walk down the access track and road to return to **Femés**.

Looking along the Valle de Femés, from the slopes of Pico de la Oveja, to Las Casitas

WALK 3
Femés to Puerto Calero

Start	Roundabout, Femés
Finish	Roundabout, Puerto Calero
Distance	12km (7½ miles)
Total Ascent	270m (885ft)
Total Descent	610m (2000ft)
Time	3hrs 30min
Terrain	Mostly clear paths, initially on steep, stony and rocky slopes. A vague stretch later, then clear cliff coast paths.
Refreshment	Bar restaurants at Femés, Playa Quemada and Puerto Calero.
Transport	Occasional buses serve Femés on weekdays from Arrecife, Playa Honda and Tías. Regular daily buses link Puerto Calero with the airport and Playa Blanca.

Apart from a rocky, stone-strewn path on a steep slope early in the walk, most of this route is easy. A descent through an empty barranco leads to the sandy beach of Playa del Pozo, then a cliff coast path leads to the village of Playa Quemada and onwards to a holiday resort and marina at Puerto Calero.

▶ The last bus stop at **Femés** is near a little supermercado. There is a nearby roundabout with a palm tree at its centre and this is where the walk starts, around 370m (1215ft). First, take a look around the village – especially the plaza, church and a mirador overlooking distant Playa Blanca and Fuerteventura. There are bar restaurants, as well as the cheese-making Quesería Rubicón. A signpost for the PR LZ 09 stands at the roundabout, pointing up a tarmac road that gives way to a track. Climb past a notice for the Monumento Natural Los Ajaches, with views of Femés and the Valle de Femés.

A goat farm is reached on a stony gap at Loma Pico de la Aceituna, at 414m (1358ft). Two mapboards and two signposts stand to the right. The PR LZ 10-11 heads left, but almost immediately turns right. ▶ A broad path,

Route uses PR LZ 10 and 11.

The PR LZ 09 heads right, followed on Walk 1 and Walk 4.

39

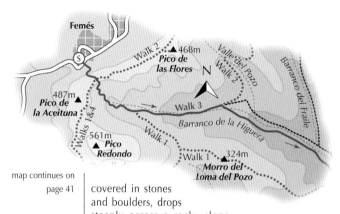

map continues on
page 41

Walk 1 joins
from the right.

covered in stones
and boulders, drops
steeply across a rocky slope
while exploiting soft beds of rock. There is
crude stone paving later, then the path swings left and
runs down to a three-way signpost in the **Barranco de la
Higuera**, around 260m (855ft). ◀

Keep left, or straight ahead through the barranco,
roughly following pylons to reach another signpost at
127m (417ft). Take careful note of where the signpost
actually points. Most walkers continue to the coast using

*A signposted path junction deep
in the Barranco de la Higuera*

the track, which is fine, but our route follows a vague
path off to the right across the stony, scrubby bed of the
barranco. Look across the bed and aim towards a drystone enclosure, then aim for another one, picking up a
narrow path that quickly becomes obvious. This eventually leads to a signpost overlooking a beach at **Playa
del Pozo**, which could easily be missed if the track was
followed. ▶ Turn left as signposted for Playa Quemada,
and a track begins to run inland towards **Barranco del
Fraile**. Follow it, but quickly turn right up a track blasted
from a rocky slope above the sea.

There is a 'pozo', or
well, on the beach.

There is a metal marker beside the track, where a path
heads off to the right, bending, rising and falling while
cutting across rocky and stony slopes. A path junction is
reached where there is a choice between zigzagging down
to the sea and climbing again, or drifting inland with less
descent and ascent. Both paths rejoin before a mapboard
is reached at the seaside village of **Playa Quemada**. Follow
roads that run close to the sea to spot a number of bar restaurants. There is a mapboard and signpost at a bus shelter
beside a road junction, but no bus services. Unless a pick-
up or taxi can be arranged, walkers need to continue along
the coast for another hour.

Walk to the far end of the village, to the end of the tarmac road, where a track continues parallel to the coast.
The track is mostly used by cyclists; walkers
might prefer
to follow
a narrow,

rugged
path near
the low cliffs of
Risco Prieto. Either way,

41

Looking along the coast to Playa Quemada, Puerto Calero and Puerto del Carmen

head towards the large **Hotel Hesperia Lanzarote**. Join a road and rise to pass the hotel entrance. When a road junction is reached turn right downhill, and the road then bends left and begins to rise. Watch on the right for a house called Gran Cortijo Viejo, where a gritty path and a few steps drop to a brick-paved promenade.

Turn left and follow the palm-fringed promenade as it runs between a **marina** and apartments. There are a couple of points where it is possible to go down to the marina, which has a range of shops, bars and restaurants, as well as a Museo de Cetacéos (whales and dolphins museum). Staying on the brick-paved path, however, cross the access road for the marina at **Puerto Calero** and continue until it passes above a boatyard. The paving ends and the path drops to a road. Turn left up the road to reach a roundabout with an attractive yacht sculpture. There is a bus shelter to the right.

WALK 4
Femés to Playa Blanca

Start	Roundabout, Femés
Finish	Avenida Marítima, Playa Blanca
Distance	23km (14¼ miles)
Total Ascent	230m (755ft)
Total Descent	600m (1970ft)
Time	7hrs
Terrain	Mountain paths traverse steep, rocky slopes, then easy tracks lead to the coast.
Refreshment	Bar restaurants at Femés. Small bar restaurants at Papagayo. Plenty of choice between Las Coloradas and Playa Blanca.
Transport	Occasional buses serve Femés on weekdays from Arrecife, Playa Honda and Tías. Plenty of buses link Las Coloradas with Playa Blanca, and Playa Blanca with Arrecife.

This long walk starts on steep, exposed slopes but later follows broad, easy tracks. After descending from the mountains, tracks run parallel to the coast, crossing several barrancos. After exploring Punta de Papagayo, easy coastal paths and promenades are followed to and through the resort of Playa Blanca.

▶ The last bus stop at **Femés** is near a little supermercado. There is a nearby roundabout with a palm tree at its centre and this is where the walk starts, around 370m (1215ft). First, take a look around the village – especially the plaza, church and a mirador overlooking distant Playa Blanca and Fuerteventura. There are bar restaurants, as well as the cheese-making Quesería Rubicón. A signpost for the PR LZ 09 stands at the roundabout, pointing up a tarmac road that gives way to a track. Climb past a notice for the Monumento Natural Los Ajaches, with views of Femés and the Valle de Femés.

A goat farm is reached on a stony gap at Loma Pico de la Aceituna, at 414m (1358ft). Two mapboards and two signposts stand to the right. The PR LZ 09 heads right,

Route uses PR LZ 09.

43

The PR LZ 10-11 heads left, followed on Walk 2 and Walk 3. ◄

and is easy to spot as it has a black plastic water pipe alongside. ◄ The path crosses the steep and rocky **Pico de la Aceituna**, and while it is technically easy to walk, you cannot afford to trip or stumble. The rock comes in pastel shades, exposed to the elements by serious over-grazing. The view down the **Barranco de la Higuera** extends along the coast to built-up resorts and distant Arrecife. Despite the steepness of the slope, the path runs gently down and up, squeezing past prickly pears at one point.

Rise and cross a stony gap at 441m (1447ft), then follow the path round the steep, rocky slopes of Pico Redondo. The water pipe still runs alongside, and views stretch towards Playa Blanca and

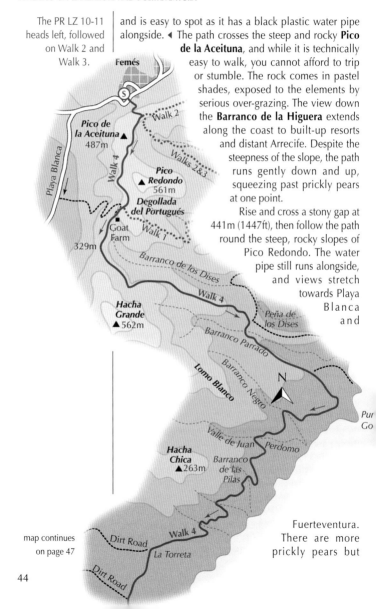

Fuerteventura. There are more prickly pears but

map continues on page 47

Walkers follow a track down from a small goat farm at Degollada del Portugués

otherwise the mountainside is bare and over-grazed. When a fork is reached, keep right and follow the path down to a track at the small goat farm at **Degollada del Portugués**, at 419m (1375ft). ▶

The path climbing left is used on Walk 1.

Turn left to follow the track down to a stony gap at 329m (1079ft), swinging left to continue down across the flanks of the **Barranco de los Dises**. The track winds downhill and later there are views of the coast stretching to Arrecife. The track forks twice; keep left both times. Reach a signposted junction at **Peña de los Dises**, at 137m (449ft). Turn right, down onto the bed of the **Barranco Parrado**. The track climbs from it, passing a marker post. Follow the track as it rises, then falls, keeping left at a junction and going straight through a track intersection. The track descends, swings round a barranco, and then rises. It does the same with three more barrancos, reaching a signpost on the Lomo **Barranco de las Pilas**, at 69m (226ft).

The track continues bending as it crosses arid, stony slopes, and also passes small quarries. Later, avoid a track descending left to the coast, and very soon afterwards, avoid a track climbing steeply to the right. Eventually a signposted junction is reached at **La Torreta**, at 59m (194ft), and there is a glimpse of Playa Blanca ahead.

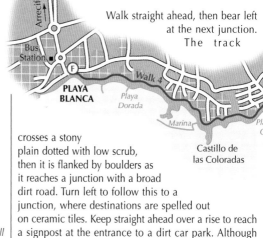

Walk straight ahead, then bear left at the next junction. The track crosses a stony plain dotted with low scrub, then it is flanked by boulders as it reaches a junction with a broad dirt road. Turn left to follow this to a junction, where destinations are spelled out on ceramic tiles. Keep straight ahead over a rise to reach a signpost at the entrance to a dirt car park. Although a signpost points right, disregard it and either bear left or straight ahead. Follow any path on the headland of **Punta de Papagayo**, to find a couple of sandy beaches

A collection of small bars above Playa de Papagayo on Punta de Papagayo

and attractive cliff-top walks. Views across the sea take in the islands of Lobos and Fuerteventura. Afterwards, head for a huddle of little bar restaurants at **Papagayo**.

Continue along the coast, either visiting the sandy beaches of **Playa del Pozo** and **Playa Mujeres**, or staying a little further inland to avoid them. Use sandy or stony paths, and either walk around headlands or short-cut behind them. The first building reached looks remarkably like a ship, then a steep, rocky descent leads to an easy promenade path beside the pebbly **Playa de las Coloradas**. The promenade ends where an old house has survived the relentless resort expansion. Pick up the promenade on the other side and pass the Gran Castillo. Next, there is access inland to a shopping centre and buses, where the walk could be finished early, saving 3km (2 miles).

The promenade runs along a cliff-top and passes the **Castillo de las Coloradas**, where there is a signpost. Go down steps towards an attractive marina development. Either hug the harbour-side or use paved paths a little further inland, but there is no need to walk on roads. ▶ Eventually, pass the Hotel Playa Dorado and walk until a tiny sandy beach is reached at **Playa Blanca**. Turn right inland on the narrow Avenida Marítima to reach the town centre and a mapboard for the PR LZ 09.

Admire the architecture, water features and planted areas around the marina; there also are plenty of places offering refreshment.

47

WALK 5

Playa Blanca to El Golfo

Start	Avenida Marítima, Playa Blanca
Finish	El Golfo
Distance	25km (15½ miles)
Total Ascent/Descent	150m (490ft)
Time	8hrs
Terrain	Easy promenade at first, then good paths, then awkward, stony areas. After a stretch of road-walking there is a short beach walk and an ash path.
Refreshment	Plenty of choice in Playa Blanca. Bar restaurants at El Golfo.
Transport	Regular daily buses serve Playa Blanca from Arrecife and the airport. A pick-up or taxi is needed at El Golfo.

Many walkers stroll along the promenade at Playa Blanca and continue across bleak and barren lava flows, wondering where it all might end. This walk includes rugged paths and roads, stretching all the way to El Golfo and taking in remarkable sights. There is no transport at the end, so a pick-up or taxi needs to be arranged.

Start at the tiny sandy beach at **Playa Blanca**, which is reached from the Avenida Marítima. Face the sea, turn right and walk past several bar restaurants. Later, two flights of steps lead down to a pebbly

map continues on page 49

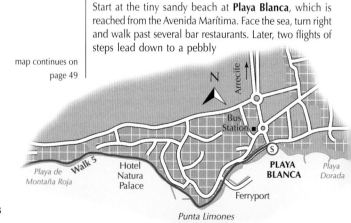

Early morning at Playa Blanca, when you can have the beach all to yourself

beach, so use either of them to join and follow a tarmac road past the **ferryport**. (You could park and start from here if you need save a few minutes walking time.) The promenade path passes bungalow apartments at Puerto Chico and then the Iberostar development, with views across the sea to the islands of Lobos and Fuerteventura. Pass a kiosk, bar restaurant and a couple of shops, then climb a little to pass a look-out/bunker. Pass the Timanfaya Palace Hotel and descend a little, crossing a footbridge over the rocky bed of a barranco. Pass the **Hotel Natura Palace**, then there is a shop inland and bar restaurants overlooking a little beach. The promenade passes the H10 Rubicón Palace, then there are lots of sun loungers belonging to the Royal Mónica on **Playa de Montaña Roja**.

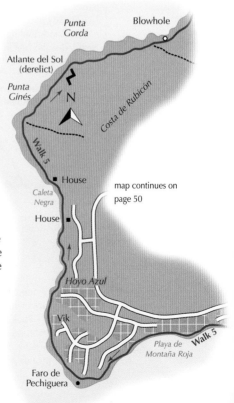

map continues on page 50

Later, there is a gap in the promenade path, then it resumes to pass a few more properties, followed by a bulldozed area awaiting the attention of developers. The paving ends abruptly, so continue along a stony path, aiming right of the tall **Faro de Pechiguera**, crossing its access road. Follow a concrete wall ahead, then step over it to follow a trodden path past boulders, linking with another promenade path. A few occupied buildings face the sea, while an abandoned development lies inland. The promenade soon ends and an easy track continues. The ground alongside is bleak and stony, dotted with boulders and tabaibal. Reach a road-end and continue along another promenade past the **Vik resort**. A final built-up area is passed, then the promenade ends at **Hoyo Azul**.

An easy track leads onwards, roughly parallel to the rugged coast, ending at a wall near a house at **Caleta Negra**. Pass the wall to follow a rugged path a short way; the track then continues, passing seawards of a ramshackle dwelling. Another wall is reached on the rugged **Punta Ginés**. Looking ahead, a prominent derelict building is seen – the **Atlante del Sol**. Rugged paths and tracks run all over the place, but none go in the right direction for long, and

map continues on page 51

Desalination Plant

walkers must cross awkward areas of stones and boulders. Pass seawards of the big eyesore and scan the terrain ahead to spot paths and tracks that offer easy passage through the stones. Don't walk too close to the sea, as there are rugged rocks that take too long to pass.

Look for a drystone shelter in this bleak and rugged landscape and an easy track leads onwards. Soon afterwards, especially if the sea is pounding into the rocky coast, watch for a twin

Piedra Alta

N

Walk 5

Los Llanos de las Maretas

Blowhole

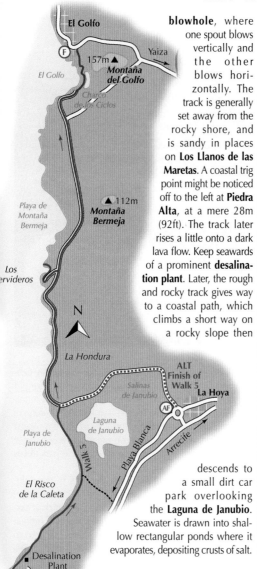

blowhole, where one spout blows vertically and the other blows horizontally. The track is generally set away from the rocky shore, and is sandy in places on **Los Llanos de las Maretas**. A coastal trig point might be noticed off to the left at **Piedra Alta**, at a mere 28m (92ft). The track later rises a little onto a dark lava flow. Keep seawards of a prominent **desalination plant**. Later, the rough and rocky track gives way to a coastal path, which climbs a short way on a rocky slope then

descends to a small dirt car park overlooking the **Laguna de Janubio**. Seawater is drawn into shallow rectangular ponds where it evaporates, depositing crusts of salt.

Los Hervideros – where the sea appears to boil furiously in caverns in a honeycombed headland

Turning right along the road allows for an early finish at La Hoya, almost 2.5km (1½ miles) away, where there are bus stops.

Here, lava flowed into the sea in the 1730s and the sea punched caverns and tunnels into the rock. A maze of paths leads to a series of splendid viewpoints.

Walk along the broad whaleback beach of grey pebbles and sand at **Playa de Janubio**, to reach a large dirt car park and a road on the other side. ◄ Turn left to follow the road across very rugged lava flows. Be careful of the traffic, and take every opportunity to explore rugged headlands and rocky chasms on the left. A few of these have lay-bys for cars, then there is a large car park at **Los Hervideros**. ◄

The road later has **Montaña Bermeja** to the right, where the lava flowed round the base of the mountain, and **Playa de Montaña Bermeja** to the left, which is easily reached if desired. When the road makes a sudden right turn, walk straight ahead along a road barred to traffic, and be careful of crumbling, overhanging cliffs

52

while walking to a beach at the end of the road. Cross the beach, looking right to see the green pool of **Charco de los Ciclos**, with dramatically sculpted, pastel-shaded cliffs above. Climb a path on loose red ash, which changes to grey as the path descends to a car park at **El Golfo**. There are plenty of bar restaurants specialising in fish dishes, as well as a small hotel and a small shop. If a taxi pick-up hasn't been arranged, retire to a bar for refreshment and ask the staff to call one. The nearest bus stops are 7km (4½ miles) inland at Yaiza.

WALK 6
Yaiza to Tinajo

Start	Aljibe, Yaiza, or Juan Perdomo
Finish	Teatro Tinajo, or Playa de la Madera
Distance	30 or 13km (18½ or 8 miles)
Total Ascent/Descent	300 or 50m (985 or 165ft)
Time	10 or 5hrs
Terrain	Easy walking on roads and dirt roads at the start and finish. Difficult, rough, rocky, stony paths in the middle of the walk.
Refreshment	Bar restaurants at Yaiza and Tinajo.
Transport	Regular daily buses serve Yaiza and Tinajo from Arrecife. To avoid lengthy road-walks at the beginning and end, arrange drop-off and pick-up.

This rugged coastal walk crosses extensive lava flows dating from the 1730s, now part of the Parque Nacional de Timanfaya. It is exceptionally rough and rocky, and cannot be hurried without risking an injury. The distance can be halved if a drop-off and pick-up is used to avoid the roads and dirt roads at the start and finish.

The nearest bus stop to the start is the 'Aljibe' at **Yaiza**. There is sometimes a taxi parked at the church, but if relying on it, book in advance. If walking all the way,

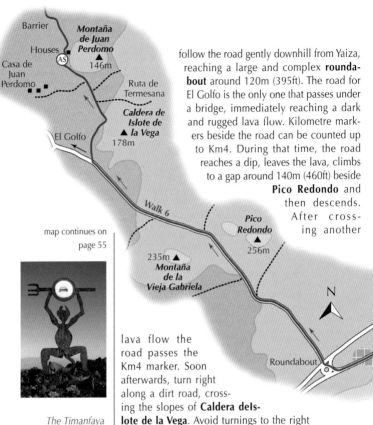

Barrier

Montaña de Juan Perdomo ▲ 146m

Houses

Casa de Juan Perdomo

Ruta de Termesana

Caldera de Islote de ▲ **la Vega** 178m

El Golfo

Walk 6

map continues on page 55

Pico Redondo ▲ 256m

235m ▲ **Montaña de la Vieja Gabriela**

N

Roundabout

The Timanfaya devil warns people off trying to drive beyond Montaña de Juan Perdomo

This would save the initial walk-in of 8km (5 miles).

follow the road gently downhill from Yaiza, reaching a large and complex **roundabout** around 120m (395ft). The road for El Golfo is the only one that passes under a bridge, immediately reaching a dark and rugged lava flow. Kilometre markers beside the road can be counted up to Km4. During that time, the road reaches a dip, leaves the lava, climbs to a gap around 140m (460ft) beside **Pico Redondo** and then descends. After crossing another lava flow the road passes the Km4 marker. Soon afterwards, turn right along a dirt road, crossing the slopes of **Caldera deIslote de la Vega**. Avoid turnings to the right into the national park (the popular, short, guided Ruta de Termesana starts here), as well as a turning to the left to the **Casa de Juan Perdomo**. Instead, walk between white concrete pillars and follow an ash track overlooking little houses, El Golfo, and distant Fuerteventura.

The track rises towards a couple of **houses**, where a drop-off is possible but there is no parking. ◄ Keep left of the houses to follow the track onwards, down past a Timanfaya 'devil' with a car symbol skewered on its fork! Enter the national park and pass a barrier. The track runs on and off lava flows, which support nothing but lichens. Areas not reached by the lava in the 1730s are generally covered in tabaibal. A short extension along the track leads to the black-sand beach of **Playa del Paso**, an additional 1km (½ mile) of walking, there-and-back. To omit this, simply turn right along a rugged path signposted for Playa del Cochino.

Although the road and dirt road might have been covered at a brisk pace, the rugged, awkward, stony path across the lava must be covered slowly and carefully. The path is narrow and has been created simply by pushing boulders to one side, leaving plenty of rough stones. If it proves too difficult, turn back before it becomes even more difficult!

Pass narrow inlets and headlands where the sea beats at the lava. The path meanders, rises and falls, and then there is an easier stretch covered in black sand and shells. It becomes more rugged again and almost vanishes while passing a **stone shelter**. If the path is lost, it is important to locate it again, and **never** short-cut across the lava, which could be hollow underfoot and collapse without warning.

Playa del Cochino cannot be mistaken, as the 'beach' is an extensive area of big, rounded boulders and grey sand, with grape-like uvilla growing. There was also, at the time of writing, a substantial **driftwood shelter**, but there is no guarantee that the national park authorities will allow it to remain. Look very carefully to spot the rugged path onwards from another stone shelter; it is scantily marked by parallel lines of small stones that aren't always easy to spot. The path crosses both ropy and blocky lava, over and over again. The only readily identifiable feature in

map continues on page 56

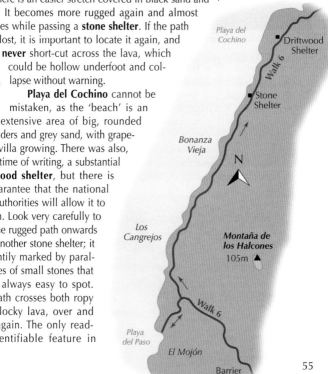

The sea beats relentlessly at a lava flow created in the 1730s. Local fishermen say that it is angry at losing so much of its domain

If a pick-up can be arranged at this point, it saves a 10.5km (6½ mile) walk to the finish.

this chaotic rock-scape is a trig point at **Paletón**. This stands at a mere 22m (72ft), but the terrain is as rugged as any mountain! Later, the path leaves the national park at a notice and then

reaches the black sand beach of **Playa de la Madera.** ◀

Follow a dirt road inland, passing a wall marked with a huge 'privado' notice. A mapboard and signpost stand at a track junction, relating to the PR LZ 19 linking the beach of **Playa de las Malvas** with the village of

Playa las M

Playa de las Madera

La Cruz (AF)

Car Park

Tabaibas

Walk 6

Paletón
22m

Bajita Blanco

56

■ Driftwood Shelter

After all the rugged lava, easy tracks and roads lead finally to the village of Tinajo

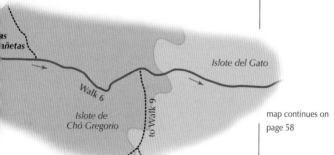

Islote del Gato

Walk 6

Islote de Chó Gregorio

to Walk 9

map continues on page 58

Mancha Blanca (but only the fittest of walkers will have the energy to follow it across more lava flows). Follow the dirt road inland and uphill on a slope of tabaibal. This gives way to a rugged lava flow, and then the **Islote de Chó Gregorio** is crossed, where there is more tabaibal and other scrub. The dirt road rises onto another lava flow and then reaches a signposted junction at 74m (243ft). The PR LZ 19 heads right, and links with Walk 9, but keep straight ahead, further inland and uphill across another lava flow.

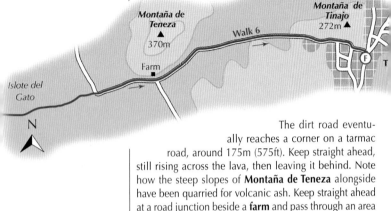

The dirt road eventually reaches a corner on a tarmac road, around 175m (575ft). Keep straight ahead, still rising across the lava, then leaving it behind. Note how the steep slopes of **Montaña de Teneza** alongside have been quarried for volcanic ash. Keep straight ahead at a road junction beside a **farm** and pass through an area of black ash fields surrounded by drystone walls. There are mountains and houses in the distance, while to the left the island of La Graciosa and its neighbours are seen briefly.

The name of the road changes, around 200m (655ft), from Camino Las Malvas to Calle La Laguneta, continuing straight ahead into the sprawling village of **Tinajo**. There are houses to the right and a heavily quarried slope to the left. The road bends right and left at junctions and continues into the village. When a junction with the main road is reached, either turn left for bus stops at the Plaza San Roque, or right for bus stops at the Teatro Tinajo.

WALK 7

Mozaga to Uga

Start	Correos, Mozaga
Finish	Church, Uga
Distance	21.5km (13½ miles)
Total Ascent	370m (1215ft)
Total Descent	430m (1410ft)
Time	7hrs
Terrain	Mostly easy walking along roads and dirt roads, only occasionally steep.
Refreshment	Hotel restaurants at Mozaga and La Florida. Small bars at El Islote, Montaña Blanca, Masdache and Conil. Bar restaurants at Uga.
Transport	Regular daily buses serve Mozaga, La Florida, Montaña Blanca, Masdache and Uga from Arrecife or Playa Honda. Occasional weekday buses serve Conil and La Asomada from Arrecife and Playa Honda.

This easy trail passes old lava flows and old volcanoes, traversing the extensive vineyards of La Geria, which are covered in black volcanic ash. Country roads and dirt roads link a handful of villages that usually feature a small bar. Bus services allow the route to be shortened, while adjacent volcanoes can be climbed as 'extras'.

▶ The PR LZ 06 starts at the Monumento al Campesino between San Bartolomé and Mozaga, but the road is too busy to walk in comfort. The first mapboard and signpost for the route have been wrongly erected at the 'Correos' bus stop at **Mozaga**, which is a much better place to start, at 260m (855ft). Take a look at the lava flow between the road and the village, which features a deep and dramatic crack and a surface covered in fleshy aeoniums. Walk to a nearby roundabout and turn left along a road signposted 'Pá Dolores' to leave the village. The road rises gently past lava and fields of black volcanic ash to reach a crossroads.

Route uses PR LZ 06.

Turn left as signposted for **El Islote**, staying on the broadest road, Calle Parral, as it bends right and left through the village. There are small cultivated plots of volcanic ash, while cracks and holes in rugged lava flows support vines or fig trees. The surface of the lava is usually covered in aeoniums and *verode*, with occasional prickly pears and aloes. Only a few buses come into the village, and the Tele Club offers the only refreshments. The road leaves the village and reaches a complex road junction beside the Finca La Florida rural **hotel**, at 286m (938ft). A triangular plaza is shaded by palm trees and there is a bus shelter. ◄

Walk 8 starts and finishes here, and can be used to vary this walk via Masdache.

Leave the road junction by following Calle Lagar, signposted as the PR LZ 06 to Guatisea. There are a few houses, and the last house on the right has converted a lava flow in its garden into crazy paving. Follow the road uphill, overlooking black ash vineyards and rugged, vegetated old lava flows. Descend to a road junction and signpost at Guatisea, around 300m (985ft). ◄ Follow the road straight ahead, passing only the topmost houses in the village of **Montaña Blanca**, at 318m (1043ft). Although there is a small bar it is almost 1km (½ mile) away at the bottom of the village.

The PR LZ 06 includes an option to climb Monte Guatisea. See Walk 8 for details.

Turn right to walk up the road, crossing a rise followed by a dip. Keep straight ahead, avoiding all turnings to left and right, and again keep straight ahead through a crossroads near **Masdache**. ◄ The road passes extensive black ash vineyards, later bending right at **Bodegas Martinón** to reach a signposted road junction. Turn left and follow the road past more vineyards, noting a turning on the left called Camino La Magdalena. However, keep straight ahead, watching for the next turning on the left, which is called Camino Entre Montañas, at 220m (720ft) at Testeina (signposted as the PR LZ 06).

Note that a right turn here quickly leads to the village and a snack bar.

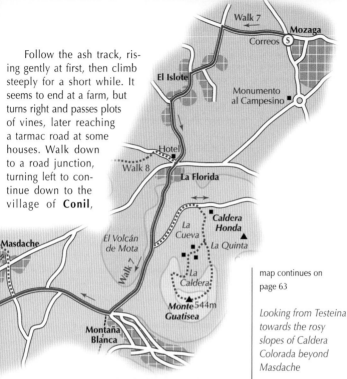

Follow the ash track, rising gently at first, then climb steeply for a short while. It seems to end at a farm, but turns right and passes plots of vines, later reaching a tarmac road at some houses. Walk down to a road junction, turning left to continue down to the village of **Conil**,

map continues on page 63

Looking from Testeina towards the rosy slopes of Caldera Colorada beyond Masdache

The GR 131, covered on Walk 20, lies a little further downhill.

at 295m (970ft). ◄ Turn right to pass the church and a snack bar, following the road past houses and later passing another little bar and a shop. The road leaves the village, overlooking slopes stretching down towards the sea, then passes a roadside **ermita** at Vega de Tegoyo. The road then rises past more vineyards, eventually reaching a junction at **Tablero**.

Turn left and follow the road over a gap around 370m (1215ft). Descend into the straggly village of **La Asomada**, passing a small supermarket and linking with the course of the long-distance GR 131. Turn right at a road junction at 315m (1035ft), as signposted for Uga, up the Camino de Caldereta; the road passes a notice drawing attention to the islands of Lobos and Fuerteventura in the distance. As the houses peter out and the road becomes a dirt road, the gentle slopes of **La Montañeta** lie to the left, while the steep slopes of **Montaña de Guardilama** rise to the right. The dirt road crosses a gentle dip then climbs a steep, scrub-covered slope to reach a gap at 419m (1375ft).

> **Montaña de Guardilama** can be climbed, using a steep and obvious path on the right, for exceptional views from its 605m (1985ft) summit. An easier circuit of **Montaña Tinasoria**, at 503m (1650ft), can be made by following a track on the left.

The dirt road descends, overlooking the extensive black ash vineyards of **La Geria**, which stretch

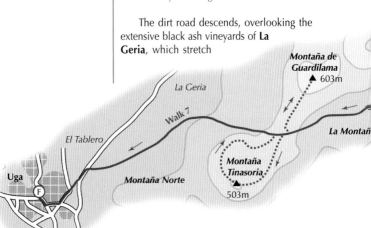

towards the grey-and-rose-coloured mountains of the Parque Nacional de Timanfaya. Thousands of pits have been excavated from the ash, each equipped with a semicircular wall to protect a single vine. The descent is steep for a while and the ash, which rained down in the 1730s, has worn in places to reveal the original ground beneath.

It is well worth climbing to the summit of Montaña de Guardilama to enjoy extensive views

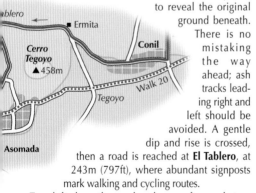

There is no mistaking the way ahead; ash tracks leading right and left should be avoided. A gentle dip and rise is crossed, then a road is reached at **El Tablero**, at 243m (797ft), where abundant signposts mark walking and cycling routes.

Turn left along the road and soon afterwards turn right down an ash track, as signposted. The village of **Uga** is in sight, sitting in a hollow completely surrounded by higher ground. At its centre is a circular, walled hole where rainwater could drain and be stored. At the bottom of the track turn left along a road and then keep right at junctions, aiming for the centre of the village, around 200m (655ft), where there is a bus shelter near a church, a supermarket and two bar restaurants.

WALK 8
Cueva de los Naturalistas

Start/Finish	La Florida
Distance	9km (5½ miles)
Total Ascent/Descent	100m (330ft)
Time	3hrs
Terrain	Mostly easy walking along roads and dirt roads. Care is needed if exploring rugged lava flows, which are riddled with cracks and holes.
Refreshment	Hotel restaurant at La Florida. Snack bar at Masdache. Small bar off-route at Montaña Blanca.
Transport	Regular daily buses serve La Florida, Masdache and Montaña Blanca from Arrecife and Playa Honda.

An extensive lava flow lies between the villages of Masdache and Mancha Blanca, with old volcanoes around it. The lava is full of caves, either in the form of holes or long tubes. The Monumento Natural Cueva de los Naturalistas can be explored, at least in part, and there is an optional extension onto Monte Guatisea.

Route uses Sendero Juan Bello, PR LZ 06 and GR 131.

Walk 7 passes here.

◄ A bus shelter stands beside a triangular plaza shaded by palm trees at **La Florida**, at 286m (938ft).

On one side of the plaza is the Finca La Florida rural hotel, while on another side is a complex road junction. ◄ Simply follow the road signposted for Los Bermejos and Sendero Juan Bello. The road passes vineyards and soon reaches a signposted junction. Turn left along an ash track signposted as a cycling route, where the Sendero Juan Bello is marked by occasional green/

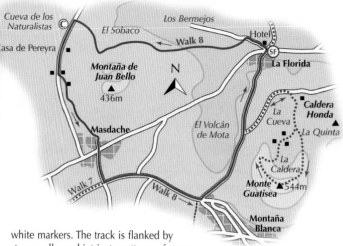

Cueva de los Naturalistas
asa de Pereyra
El Sobaco
Los Bermejos
Walk 8
Hotel
SF
La Florida
Montaña de Juan Bello
436m
N
Caldera Honda
La Cueva
La Quinta
Masdache
El Volcán de Mota
La Caldera
Monte Guatisea ▲544m
Walk 7
Walk 8 →
Montaña Blanca

white markers. The track is flanked by stone walls, and intricate patterns of stone walls have been built in black ash fields to protect vines from winds. Stay on the clearest track throughout, avoiding other tracks to left and right, and eventually there is a gentle rise to a track intersection on the lower slopes of **Montaña de Juan Bello**, around 230m (755ft).

Turn right down an ash track, which then steps up a little onto what appears to be a 'sea' of lava, complete with 'waves'. The surface is often smooth or ropy, but there are also long, wide cracks, ridges and depressions, often covered in lichen and aeoniums. The track is rather vague in places, despite having been used by vehicles. Head towards a tarmac road that isn't immediately obvious until road signs become apparent. Join the road near a 'bend' sign, but turn left away from it, then watch for a track heading to the right onto extensive lava flows from the Volcán de Tizalaya.

The track looks safe to follow, but note that it immediately runs across the top of a cave, whose openings can be seen to either side, and whose interior, at the time of writing, was furnished! Feel free to observe the lava flows from the track, but if tempted to walk across the surface beware of deep cracks and holes, and bear in mind that you could be standing on a thin crust of lava above a deep and dangerous hole. If the

Buckled and fractured lava can be studied near the Cueva de los Naturalistas

surface were to break, you would instantly vanish and probably suffer serious injury. With these warnings in mind, continue along the tarmac road, heading roughly southwards and passing a pair of 'no overtaking' signs. Another track on the right quickly leads to an impressive collapsed lava tube, the **Cueva de los Naturalistas**, with boulder-choked caves at either end. If exploring close to this feature, or if tempted inside it, bear in mind the ever-present danger of rockfall.

Continue along the tarmac road, passing a house called **Casa de Pereyra** and then more houses on both sides of the road. When the road has no houses alongside, turn left along an ash track, which quickly turns right and passes a couple of houses and later a sports ground. This track leads onto a road, which in turn leads straight to a crossroads in the village of **Masdache**, where there is a bus shelter and a snack bar, around 310m (1020ft). Walk straight ahead through the crossroads, leaving the village and passing black ash vineyards to reach another crossroads. ◀ Turn left and follow the road, crossing a dip and then climbing gently over a rise before dropping towards the topmost houses at **Montaña Blanca**, at 318m

Walk 7 is joined here.

(1043ft). There is a small bar, but it is almost 1km (½ mile) away at the bottom of the village.

Turn left along a road, as signposted for the PR LZ 06 to Guatisea, and follow it down to a road junction, overlooking black ash vineyards and rugged, vegetated old lava flows. Keep left at another signposted junction (from which point an extension to Monte Guatisea is possible), rising and falling to return to the complex road junction at **La Florida**.

Extension to Monte Guatisea

This optional visit to the top of Monte Guatisea adds 5km (3 miles) in length and 245m (805ft) of ascent and descent to the original route. From the last signposted road junction, turn right and follow the road uphill. It bends right and eventually reaches a signpost for the long-distance GR 131. Turn right along a track, pass a marker for Km37, and turn left at a track junction at **La Quinta**. When a marker post is reached, simply look uphill and spot a vague path climbing steeply up a ridge. The gradient eases later, as the ridge swings gradually right to reach the top of **Monte Guatisea**, at 544m (1785ft). ▶

Views embrace the whole of Lanzarote and stretch even further, to the islands of La Graciosa and Fuerteventura.

An extension to the walk can include a steep climb to the summit of Monte Guatisea for fine views

For the descent, either retrace steps or continue around the ridge. If taking the latter course, watch carefully to spot a path on the right, cutting across steep, vegetated slopes inside the crater, then head down to link with an access track that passes a farm. This returns to a junction passed earlier in the walk, rejoining the GR 131. Follow it back to the road, where left and right turns at junctions lead to **La Florida**.

WALK 9
Mancha Blanca and Caldera Blanca

Start/Finish	Mancha Blanca
Distance	21 or 24km (13 or 15 miles)
Total Ascent/Descent	230 or 480m (755 or 1575ft)
Time	6 or 7hrs
Terrain	Rugged, stony paths across lava flows, followed by optional steep paths at Caldera Blanca. Easy dirt roads and a tarmac road later.
Refreshment	Bar restaurant at Mancha Blanca.
Transport	Regular daily buses link Mancha Blanca with Arrecife and La Santa.

Caldera Blanca is a huge volcanic crater, over 1km (½ mile) in diameter, in the Parque Natural de los Volcanes. It can be approached by crossing a lava flow, then walkers may pass it, climb it, descend into its crater or walk round its rim. Dirt roads and a tarmac road lead to the national park visitor centre.

Route uses PR LZ 19.

◀ Start at the bus stops at **Mancha Blanca**, around 280m (920ft). Follow the road in the direction of Tinajo and turn left as signposted for Timanfaya. Pass a shop and bar restaurant while following the road out of the village, avoiding left turns that lead back among the houses. The road passes black ash fields and then bends left at a junction. At this point, **El Tablero**, a signpost for the PR LZ 19 points along a dirt road. Follow it, keeping straight ahead at a junction while passing fields, then step up a little onto a rugged lava flow. The dirt road ends at a small car park, where motorists can save themselves 1.5km (1 mile) of walking. ▶

Continue along a stony path, where boulders have been pushed aside. The path descends into a rugged hollow and then rises and continues, with only occasional spiky clumps of aulaga alongside. Later, reach a well-vegetated margin between the lava and the slopes of **Montaña Caldereta**, where the path runs around the base of an old volcano. The crater wall has a significant breach, allowing it to be entered with ease.

> Crumbling structures and a well indicate that the **fertile ground** was formerly used by farmers. Montaña Caldereta, like other nearby volcanoes, is an 'islote', or 'island' of fertile ground surrounded by the sterile 1730s lava.

There are two ways to continue, depending on whether walkers want to walk past Caldera Blanca or walk round its crater rim and climb to its summit. The former is short and easy, measuring only 1km (½ mile), while the latter is

The lava dates from the 1730s and is barren apart from a crust of lichen, but vegetation grows beside the track where the ground has been disturbed.

Montaña Caldereta sits in a vast expanse of rugged lava near Mancha Blanca

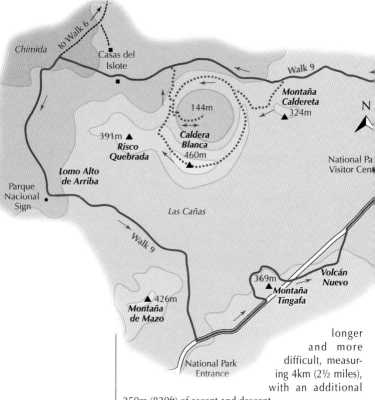

longer
and more
difficult, measur-
ing 4km (2½ miles),
with an additional
250m (820ft) of ascent and descent.

To pass the *caldera*, follow a path that runs back onto
the rugged lava, and later keep right at a path junction.
The path leaves the lava at a signpost, where a right turn
leads gently down a track around the base of **Caldera
Blanca**, below 200m (655ft). The steep slopes above are
riven with small gullies, while plants such as straggly
'tobacco' trees, tabaibal and aulaga grow on the more
stable parts. The track swings left and climbs over a gentle
gap at 150m (490ft).

> To explore and climb around the caldera, fol-
> low a path that rises around the lower slopes of
> **Montaña Caldereta**, staying well above the rugged

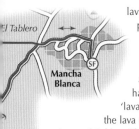

lava flows. However, the path later crosses the lava where it flowed between two mountains in the 1730s and formed what must have been an awesome 'lava-fall'. The path leaves the lava and continues onto the slopes of **Caldera Blanca**. It is trodden deep into the slope, but otherwise rises easily to a point on the crater rim, just below 300m (985ft). ▶ Turn left to follow the crater rim to the summit, where there is a trig point at 460m (1509ft). Views are extensive, and there are straggly 'tobacco' trees growing. Follow the ridge onwards, with a little more care, to reach the lowest point on the crater rim at 253m (830ft).It is possible to descend to the right, deep into the **crater**, whose lowest point is 144m (472ft), then climb back.

Locate a path descending to the left, which leads down to a track on a gentle gap over 150m (490ft).

The crater is an amazing sight, if only because of its size and uniform circular shape.

The national park visitor centre is buried in rugged lava, with Caldera Blanca rising beyond

The PR LZ 19 can be followed right, along dirt roads, to reach the coast at Playa de las Malvas.

Follow the track gently downhill, flanked by walls as it passes through a gentle area featuring a few fields. A house is seen on the right, embedded in lava, then there is suddenly a house immediately to the left at **Casas del Islote**. The track runs onwards, then steps up a little onto the rugged lava, reaching a signposted junction at **Chimida**, at 89m (292ft). ◄ Turn left to follow a track gently uphill, crossing rugged lava flows and spotting areas alongside where the original fertile slopes avoided being covered, and so generally feature vegetation.

Keep straight ahead at a junction and keep rising, with the track surface becoming more rugged. There is a sudden left turn at a 'Parque Nacional' sign (it is forbidden to walk on the lava beyond). As the track continues its gradual ascent, there are occasional *calcosas* bushes alongside. The slopes of Caldera Blanca rise to the left, and later the ash slopes of **Montaña de Mazo** to the right. Join a road at almost 300m (985ft) and turn left to follow it, passing a Timanfaya 'devil' while walking from the Km13 marker to Km12. The road can be followed directly to the national park visitor centre and Mancha Blanca, but it is dead straight and traffic races along, so walkers might wish to avoid it.

When the road runs close to the foot of **Montaña Tingafa** at Km12, watch for a path heading left, crossing rugged lava well away from the foot of the little mountain. At first it appears that the path is going the wrong way, but after turning right at a junction it reaches the foot of the mountain, joining an ash track that can be followed back to the road. Cross the road and follow an ash path towards the hill of **Volcán Nuevo**, passing left of it along a stony track. This later drifts left, back to the road, and then the road is followed from the Km10 marker to the **national park visitor centre** (free access) and onwards to return to **Mancha Blanca**.

NORTH LANZAROTE

Black ash fields and volcanos feature around the village of Tinajo (Walk 10)

Lanzarote divides neatly into two halves where a broad, sandy gap stretches across the middle of the island. The former capital, Teguise, overlooks this gap, and is busiest during its Sunday market. Windblown sand migrates across the gap from the west coast at Caleta de Famara, so little is seen of the underlying rock.

Walks 10, 11 and 12 converge on Caleta de Famara, each experiencing a different part of the sandy expanse of El Jable. Walk 13 climbs a small volcano from Costa Teguise, and Walk 14 runs from Teguise to the east coast at Los Cocoteros and then heads back inland to Guatiza, which is surrounded by prickly pears and features the splendid Jardín de Cactus. Walk 15 runs from the east coast to the west coast, from Arrieta to Caleta de Famara, passing close to the highest ground on Lanzarote. Walk 16 explores one of the most northerly parts of the island, picking its way down, and back up, the steep and rugged cliffs of Risco de Famara.

Three notable features that should be visited in the north of Lanzarote include the Mirador del Río and the enormous lava tubes of Cueva de los Verodes and Jameos del Agua.

EL JABLE

Two signposted walking routes, Walk 10 and Walk 11, cross the sandy landscape of El Jable, both passing through the village of Sóo on the way to the coast at Caleta de Famara, and they are quite different to each other. Both could be varied by switching from one to the other at Sóo, and both are best avoided when strong winds cause sandstorms. Walk 12 is a shorter walk which approaches Caleta from the pretty village of Teguise.

WALK 10
Tinajo, Sóo and Caleta de Famara

Start	Plaza de San Roque, Tinajo
Finish	Caleta de Famara
Distance	15km (9½ miles)
Total Ascent	20m (65ft)
Total Descent	240m (790ft)
Time	4hrs 30min
Terrain	Clear tracks and paths across gentle sandy slopes.
Refreshment	Bar restaurants at Tinajo, Sóo and Caleta de Famara.
Transport	Regular daily buses link Tinajo with Arrecife and La Santa and link Caleta de Famara with Sóo, Teguise and Arrecife.

Introduction needed for Walk 10 here...Introduction needed for Walk 10 here...Introduction needed for Walk 10 here...Introduction needed for Walk 10 here...Introduction needed for Walk 10 here...Introduction needed for Walk 10 here...

Route uses PR LZ 20.

◄ **Tinajo** is a sprawling settlement, and this walk starts at the Plaza de San Roque where there is a church, bar, café/bakery and a bank with an ATM. The plaza has some fine trees, including three dragon trees. A mapboard and

signpost for the PR LZ 20 stand across the road from the church, at almost 200m (655ft). Walk past a roundabout in the direction of La Santa, but quickly turn right down a quieter road. Pass a small sports ground, reach a junction with Calle Higuera and turn left. Go straight through a crossroads, noting an old windmill stump to the left. Keep right at the next junction, and as the road bends left, turn right down a road that quickly becomes a dirt road. The view stretches from Peñas del Chache to La Graciosa and its neighbouring islands.

A sandy track is followed away from Tinajo, across the broad, sandy expanse of El Jable

Keep straight ahead between black ash fields surrounded by stone walls. The dirt road runs straight across a stony, sandy area, passing a **farm**. Continue across a gentle dip and then keep straight ahead, rising past track junctions and fields. Fork left along the Camino

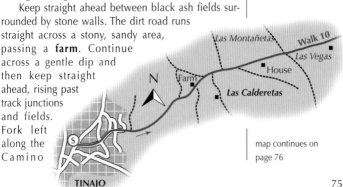

map continues on page 76

75

Right is the Camino Montañetas to the village of Muñique.

de Famara. ◄ Pass a house and continue straight ahead, avoiding all turnings to the left. Reach a signpost and track intersection at **Las Vegas**, at 139m (456ft). Again, keep straight ahead, passing a farm and, later, another structure hidden behind a stone wall. Further along, pass a **house** and go through

another track intersection before crossing a dip to reach a signpost near a road at **Las Melianas**, at 127m (417ft).

Turn left and follow an obvious track running roughly parallel to the road across **Las Peñas de San Roque**, with a village in view ahead. When a complex track junction is reached later, simply keep right towards the village and then pass through a track intersection to reach a road outside the village. Turn left, pass a bus shelter and quickly reach a road junction facing a small bar, Bodegón La Entrada, in the middle of **Sóo**, around 100m (330ft). ◄ Turn right at this junction, then right again at another junction where a signpost has been planted with some wrong directions. ◄ Walk towards a little church outside the village, keeping left of it and walking off the end of the tarmac onto a dirt road. The dirt road immediately forks, so keep left, pass the last few fields and leave the village.

Keep straight ahead along the clearest and most obvious dirt road across **La Vega del Revolcadero**. Later, cross a

There are two little shops in the village.

Walk 11 continues straight ahead at this junction.

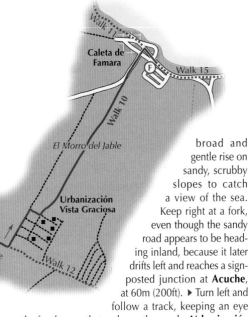

broad and gentle rise on sandy, scrubby slopes to catch a view of the sea. Keep right at a fork, even though the sandy road appears to be heading inland, because it later drifts left and reaches a signposted junction at **Acuche**, at 60m (200ft). ▶ Turn left and follow a track, keeping an eye

Walk 12 is joined here.

on the few houses that make up the nearby **Urbanización Vista Graciosa**. Turn right along a track that appears to head between the last two houses, but before reaching them turn left along another track. This runs very gently down a sandy, scrubby slope, and while it sometimes splits it rejoins further along and eventually reaches a road near some houses.

Simply follow the road straight into the seaside village of **Caleta de Famara**, reaching a crossroads and bus shelter. Walk straight ahead to the next road junction, where there are mapboards and signposts, then turn right to walk along the main street, passing bars, restaurants and shops to reach another bus shelter (which is a better place to wait for buses than the other shelter). The beach is a few paces away and is exceedingly popular with surfers, offering views of the dramatic cliffs of Risco de Famara.

WALK 11

Tiagua, Sóo and Caleta de Famara

Start	Church, Tiagua
Finish	Caleta de Famara
Distance	16km (10 miles)
Total Ascent	20m (65ft)
Total Descent	220m (720ft)
Time	5hrs
Terrain	Clear tracks and paths across gentle sandy slopes, ending with a coastal walk.
Refreshment	Bar restaurants at Tiagua, Sóo and Caleta de Famara.
Transport	Regular daily buses link Tiagua, Sóo and Caleta de Famara with Teguise and Arrecife.

Like Walk 10, this route makes its way across the sandy landscapes of El Jable to the village of Sóo on its way to the coast. Surprisingly, it looks quite different, initially passing areas that have been exploited for sand, then heading towards a rugged coastline and following it to the popular surfing village of Caleta de Famara.

Route uses PR LZ 05.

◄ If arriving on the bus for La Santa, start by taking the road from **Tiagua** towards Muñique and Sóo. If arriving

Approaching Sóo, where sandy fields give way to the slopes of Pico Colorado and Caldera Trasera

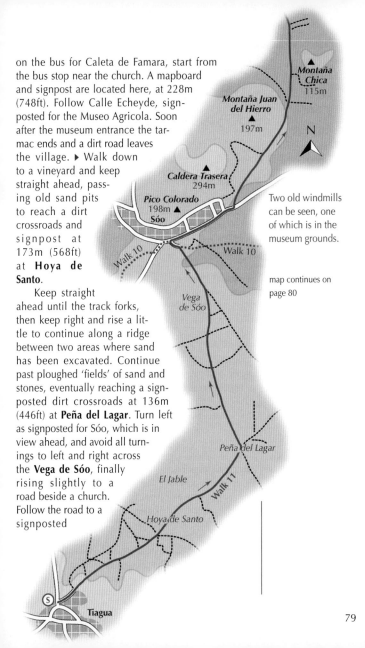

on the bus for Caleta de Famara, start from the bus stop near the church. A mapboard and signpost are located here, at 228m (748ft). Follow Calle Echeyde, signposted for the Museo Agricola. Soon after the museum entrance the tarmac ends and a dirt road leaves the village. ▶ Walk down to a vineyard and keep straight ahead, passing old sand pits to reach a dirt crossroads and signpost at 173m (568ft) at **Hoya de Santo**.

Keep straight ahead until the track forks, then keep right and rise a little to continue along a ridge between two areas where sand has been excavated. Continue past ploughed 'fields' of sand and stones, eventually reaching a signposted dirt crossroads at 136m (446ft) at **Peña del Lagar**. Turn left as signposted for Sóo, which is in view ahead, and avoid all turnings to left and right across the **Vega de Sóo**, finally rising slightly to a road beside a church. Follow the road to a signposted

Montaña Chica
115m

Montaña Juan del Hierro
197m

N

Caldera Trasera
294m

Pico Colorado
198m ▲
Sóo

Walk 10

Walk 10

Two old windmills can be seen, one of which is in the museum grounds.

map continues on page 80

Vega de Sóo

Peña del Lagar

El Jable

Walk 11

Hoya de Santo

Ⓢ
Tiagua

79

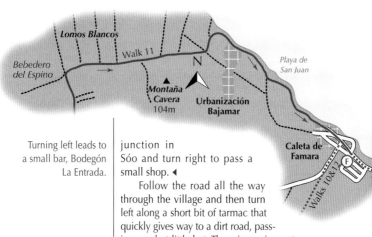

Turning left leads to a small bar, Bodegón La Entrada.

junction in Sóo and turn right to pass a small shop. ◄

Follow the road all the way through the village and then turn left along a short bit of tarmac that quickly gives way to a dirt road, passing one last little hut. There is no signpost for this turning, although there is a marker post. Keep right at a junction, then pass sandy and stony areas of scrub and fields. Eventually, reach a signposted track intersection at 100m (330ft). Note that at the time of writing this signpost was in the wrong position, and was therefore pointing the wrong way! Do not turn right as indicated down a track on a scrubby slope, but fork right, heading directly northwards. Don't take any other right turns, but descend gently until another signposted dirt crossroads is reached at **Bebedero del Espino**, at 40m (130ft).

Mapboards at Tiagua and Caleta de Famara show a route between the houses, but there are lots of 'private' notices.

Turn right and walk straight ahead past several junctions, noticing houses further ahead. ◄ Follow a track towards the coast, stepping off it to pick up a rugged path close to the rocky shore. This path passes seaward of houses at the **Urbanización Bajamar**, passing an old signpost along the way. Either continue along the coast or use paths a little further inland to reach a beach car park at **Playa de San Juan**. Follow the coast to reach the first few buildings at **Caleta de Famara**. Either stay on the coast or drift inland along dirt streets or the tarmac road through the village. The latter reaches mapboards and signposts, then passes bars, restaurants and shops to reach a bus shelter. The beach is only a few paces away and is exceedingly popular with surfers, offering views of the dramatic cliffs of Risco de Famara.

WALK 12
Teguise to Caleta de Famara

Start	Windmill, Teguise
Finish	Caleta de Famara
Distance	11km (6¾ miles)
Total Ascent	20m (65ft)
Total Descent	320m (1050ft)
Time	3hrs
Terrain	Mostly downhill, from hills to coast, along clear dirt roads and tracks.
Refreshment	Plenty of choice at Teguise and Caleta de Famara.
Transport	Regular daily buses serve Teguise and Caleta de Famara from Arrecife.

Teguise is well worth exploring, and if it takes longer than expected, this walk is short and simple, mainly following dirt roads and tracks downhill. Fine views are available on the descent, then gentle, sandy, scrubby slopes are easily crossed on the way to the coast. Caleta de Famara is popular with surfers and has good bus services.

▶ A prominent old windmill, complete with sails, over-looks a huge paved plaza behind the church in **Teguise**,

Route uses PR LZ 03.

A splendid open space lies behind the church and narrow streets of Teguise

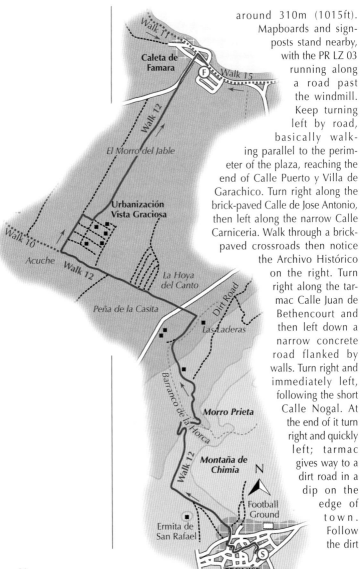

around 310m (1015ft). Mapboards and signposts stand nearby, with the PR LZ 03 running along a road past the windmill. Keep turning left by road, basically walking parallel to the perimeter of the plaza, reaching the end of Calle Puerto y Villa de Garachico. Turn right along the brick-paved Calle de Jose Antonio, then left along the narrow Calle Carniceria. Walk through a brick-paved crossroads then notice the Archivo Histórico on the right. Turn right along the tarmac Calle Juan de Bethencourt and then left down a narrow concrete road flanked by walls. Turn right and immediately left, following the short Calle Nogal. At the end of it turn right and quickly left; tarmac gives way to a dirt road in a dip on the edge of town. Follow the dirt road straight ahead at junctions, noting the hilltop **Ermita de San Rafael** away to the left. ▸

The dirt road passes a signpost at 301m (987ft) on a broad, gentle gap between low hills. Keep straight ahead for a gradual descent, bending right and overlooking a sandy plain and distant villages, with views of La Graciosa and neighbouring islands. The dirt road makes a sweeping zigzag on a steep slope and then enters and leaves the **Barranco de la Horca**. Watch on the left to spot an old, stony track leading down to a white house. Pass left of the house and follow its access track down to a track intersection. Turn right and follow a track towards buildings at **Las Laderas**, keeping left of them and then turning left down a dirt access road. Reach a tarmac road and signpost at 109m (358ft).

Cross over the road and continue straight along another dirt road. This crosses a gentle dip then rises past a road network constructed for a development that never happened. Keep straight ahead along the dirt road until a signpost is reached at a junction at **Acuche**, at 60m (200ft). ▸ Turn left and follow a track, keeping an eye on the few houses that make up the nearby **Urbanización Vista Graciosa**. Turn right along a track that appears to head between the last two houses, but before reaching them turn left along another track. This runs very gently down a sandy, scrubby slope, and while it sometimes splits, it rejoins further along, eventually reaching a road near some houses.

Simply follow the road straight into the seaside village of **Caleta de Famara**, reaching a crossroads and bus shelter. Walk straight ahead to the next road junction, where there are mapboards and signposts, then turn right to walk along the main street, passing bars, restaurants and shops to reach another bus shelter (which is a better place to wait for buses than the other shelter). The beach is a few paces away and is exceedingly popular with surfers, offering views of the dramatic cliffs of Risco de Famara.

This could be visited by making a detour off-route.

Walk 10 is joined here.

WALK 13
Costa Teguise and Montaña Tinagauche

Start/Finish	Los Zocos Club Resort, Costa Teguise
Distance	7km (4½ miles)
Total Ascent/Descent	230m (755ft)
Time	2hrs
Terrain	Mostly easy paths, but the higher slopes are steep, rocky, exposed and unsuitable for vertigo sufferers.
Refreshment	Plenty of choice in Costa Teguise
Transport	Regular daily buses serve Costa Teguise from Arrecife.

Most people wandering through the resort of Costa Teguise will see only one mountain rising inland. This is Montaña Tinaguache, although many maps give it other names. It can be climbed in a morning or afternoon, but bear in mind that its slopes are steep and rocky, and the summit ridge could be dangerous in strong winds.

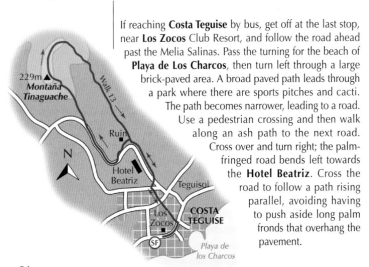

If reaching **Costa Teguise** by bus, get off at the last stop, near **Los Zocos** Club Resort, and follow the road ahead past the Melia Salinas. Pass the turning for the beach of **Playa de Los Charcos**, then turn left through a large brick-paved area. A broad paved path leads through a park where there are sports pitches and cacti. The path becomes narrower, leading to a road. Use a pedestrian crossing and then walk along an ash path to the next road. Cross over and turn right; the palm-fringed road bends left towards the **Hotel Beatriz**. Cross the road to follow a path rising parallel, avoiding having to push aside long palm fronds that overhang the pavement.

After a steep climb, a narrow path leads around a half-moon crater rim on Montaña Tinaguache

The road turns left, while the path turns right. However, keep left at the next couple of path junctions to climb onto a rocky outcrop crowned by a graffiti-splattered ruin. Pass the ruin, drop down a short, steep, stony path and continue walking parallel to the road. Later the path crosses the road, but turn right instead. ▶ Follow the pavement and road gently uphill, and when the road bends left follow a track heading right, rising towards the rugged little mountain. Pass a cairn and look carefully at the steep, rocky, barren slopes. There is a worn, uneven path with stone-strewn stretches and holes. Use hands where necessary and guard against tripping or slipping. The summit of **Montaña Tinaguache** is bare rock at 229m (751ft).

Enjoy the view and then follow the uneven, narrow, rocky summit ridge. The mountain embraces a semicircular crater with an open mouth to the south. A path descends a steep and stony slope, passing a big cairn. Continue down to a level, stony, scrubby area that is threaded by a network of paths. Keep to the most well-trodden path, passing through gaps in drystone walls and following a drystone wall over a rise, so that the resort is seen again. Simply follow the path back towards the road at the **Hotel Beatriz** and retrace steps to **Costa Teguise**.

The path makes a circuit around the resort.

WALK 14
Teguise to Guatiza

Start	Windmill, Teguise
Finish	Bar El Bulín, Guatiza
Distance	18km (11 miles)
Total Ascent	220m (720ft)
Total Descent	430m (1410ft)
Time	5hrs 30min
Terrain	Mostly easy roads and tracks. Mostly downhill, apart from short climbs at the start and finish.
Refreshment	Plenty of choice at Teguise. Bar restaurants at Guatiza.
Transport	Regular daily buses serve Teguise, Teseguite and Guatiza from Arrecife. Occasional weekday buses serve El Mojón from Arrecife.

Apart from an initial climb on the slopes of Guanapay, this route runs downhill from village to village, reaching the coast at Los Cocoteros and finishing at Guatiza. It passes agricultural areas and old ash quarries, and includes a detour to see an interesting *salina*, or salt-pan. The Jardín de Cactus can be visited at the finish.

Route uses PR LZ 04.

◄ A prominent old windmill, complete with sails, overlooks a huge paved plaza behind the church in **Teguise**, around 310m (1015ft). Mapboards and signposts stand nearby, with the PR LZ 04 running along a road towards a hill crowned by a small castle. Follow the road, Calle Garajonay, crossing a main road to pick up and follow a road marked for the **Castillo de Santa Bárbara**. ◄ Follow the road past a barrier, up ochre-coloured slopes riven by water-worn gullies. Aulaga flanks the road at first, then tabaibal and verode. A signpost is reached on the higher slopes of **Guanapay**, at 396m (1299ft), pointing along a track veering right from the road.

Notices at the start of this road explain how the castle serves as a pirate museum.

The road leads to the castle, and a **circuit** can be made around the crater rim to the 446m (1463ft) summit, returning to this point in 1.5km (1 mile).

The Castillo de Santa Barbára sits on top of Guanapay, high above Teguise

The track runs level past a hut made of lava blocks, passing fields of black ash. The track turns right and overlooks Teseguite, then turns left at a junction and descends, later joining a road beside houses. Keep straight ahead along the road, which broadens and has a palm tree in its middle. Reach a road junction between a cemetery and a church with a palm-shaded plaza on the outskirts of **Teseguite**, at 287m (942ft). Turn right and walk down the road until it bends right, then there are two roads on the left. Neither is signposted, but one bears an inconspicuous PR LZ marker on a wall. Follow the road gently downhill and walk straight ahead at a junction, keeping right of a white house.

Walk straight ahead along an ash track, following it straight across the partially cultivated plain of **Los Llanos de Teseguite**. Eventually the track bends right and passes through a complex track intersection. There are a couple of marker posts confirming the route; rise and walk straight ahead at two more junctions. Almost immediately after the second one, turn right as marked down a stony, bendy track. Climb through another track intersection,

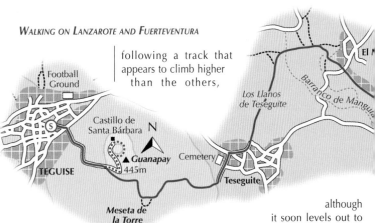

following a track that appears to climb higher than the others,

although it soon levels out to approach the village of **El Mojón**. Reach a road junction and signpost beside the Ermita de San Sebastián, at 262m (860ft), where there is a small social centre and occasional buses.

Strange 'sculptures' remain where volcanic ash has been excavated near Los Roferos

Walk straight down a road, continuing beyond the last house along an ash track. When this turns right, keep straight ahead down a rugged old track flanked by tumbled walls, on a slope dotted with verode and aulaga. Walk on bedrock at times, reaching a junction in the bed of the **Barranco de Manguía**. Turn right and follow the track up past a building, joining a road at a signpost at **Los Roferos**, at 185m (607ft). Turn left to walk gently down the road, or walk beside it wherever there is a path or track.

> The road passes an area that has been quarried for volcanic ash, and strange little towers of ash have been left standing. Two quarried mountains dominate the area – nearby **Montaña de Guenia**, and more distant **Montaña Tinamala**.

When a road junction is reached, the route becomes uncertain. A marker post on the left suggests that an old, disintegrating road is followed towards a distant white house, but there are no further markers and it is difficult to get back on course. It is easier to turn left along a dead-straight road, follow it to a roundabout and then go through a tunnel to reach another roundabout and a **filling station** at Los Cascajos. Just beyond is a roadside signpost, at 118m (387ft), pointing right along a dirt road. ▶

If time is running out, the tarmac road leads straight to Guatiza, but it is uncomfortably busy with traffic.

Follow the dirt road across a scrubby slope at the foot of **Montaña Tinamala**. The ground becomes quite bare. A signpost stands at a junction at 95m (310ft); turn left along a lesser track and follow it gently downhill, bearing left at junctions as it heads towards the coast, and later towards some distant white houses. There are deep holes in the ash, some filled with tabaibal. Keep following the track,

The PR LZ 04 turns left here, but a detour to the coast is well worthwhile.

later keeping right at junctions near a few houses, to reach a broad dirt road. ◄ Turn right along the dirt road and then left to reach the rocky coast. Turn left again to come to a coastal path beside interesting old salt-pans, the **Salinas de los Agujeros**, passing heaps of solidified salt. Small clumps of uvilla grow among the rocks, but little else. Pass houses on top of the low cliff (if the sea is pounding into the rock there may be a blowhole spouting spray).

Ahead lies **Los Cocoteros**, but turn left inland by road, reaching a signposted junction at **Vegueta del Espino**. Turn right to follow the road, passing a lay-by where there is a palm tree and clumps of tabaibal. The road climbs past old ash quarries, then prickly pears fill fields on either side as the village of **Guatiza** is entered. The road levels out near a sports ground, then the route turns right along a road bearing a 'no entry' sign. This is Calle Vicente Guerra. Another right turn marked as 'no entry' leads straight to a church; turn left to walk away from its front door, across cobbled paving. Walk straight along a street to reach the main road, where there is an avenue of eucalyptus trees. ◄

A bus shelter and a couple of bar restaurants are available. There are also shops, a post office and an ATM in the village.

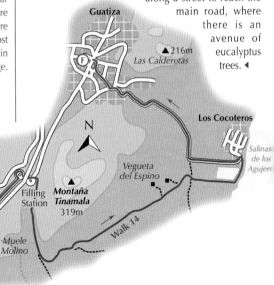

90

JARDÍN DE CACTUS

The 'cactus garden' lies outside Guatiza, beside the road heading north. A rocky hollow was developed by the artist César Manrique into an imaginative garden filled with winding paths and steps, where terraces were planted with thousands of cacti. There is a windmill above the site, as well as a bar restaurant and souvenir shop selling live cacti to anyone who wants to start their own garden. The surrounding fields are thickly planted with prickly pears, which were grown for their fruit and for rearing cochineal beetles, whose crimson body fluids were 'harvested' for cosmetics and food colouring.

WALK 15
Arrieta to Caleta de Famara

Start	Arrieta
Finish	Caleta de Famara
Distance	18.5km (11½ miles)
Total Ascent/Descent	650m (2130ft)
Time	6hrs
Terrain	A coastal path and road-walk at first, then a steep climb on a stony, scrub-covered slope. Higher tracks and roads are easy. The descent sometimes follows a rugged, narrow path on a steep slope.
Refreshment	Plenty of choice at Arrieta and Caleta de Famara. Restaurant off-route at Los Helechos.
Transport	Regular daily buses serve Arrieta and Caleta de Famara from Arrecife and Teguise.

This coast-to-coast route crosses the northern half of Lanzarote. Apart from the initial steep climb it is a fairly easy walk, passing close to the highest part of the island at Peñas del Chache. The descent uses scenic, narrow paths on steep slopes, ending with an easy walk to the seaside village of Caleta de Famara.

▶ Start in the seaside village of **Arrieta**, at a road junction near the Superservicio Arrieta. There are a number of bar restaurants nearby. Follow the road signposted 'Beach',

Route uses PR LZ 01.

which quickly leads to **Playa La Garita**. From here the copper radome (dome housing a radar dish) on the highest part of Lanzarote, Peñas del Chache,

map continues on
page 95

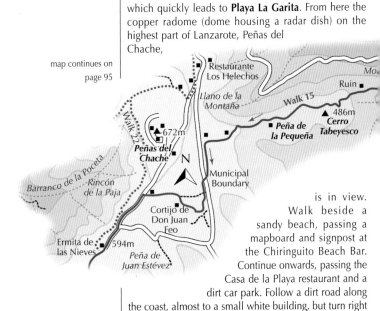

is in view. Walk beside a sandy beach, passing a mapboard and signpost at the Chiringuito Beach Bar. Continue onwards, passing the Casa de la Playa restaurant and a dirt car park. Follow a dirt road along the coast, almost to a small white building, but turn right to a signpost. The directions are vague; head towards the main road and pass beneath it using a **tunnel**. Drift to the right across a scrub-covered slope, then join a road and turn left to follow it gradually up to **Tabayesco**. ◄

It is possible to start this walk at the 'Tabayesco' bus stop on the main road, saving the first 1.5km (1 mile) of walking.

Keep left at a road junction to climb through the village, passing a little church, and walk straight through a crossroads where there is a signpost. The road leaves the village and bends sharply left and right as it climbs to around 140m (460ft). Watch carefully on the left to spot a marker post, where a vague path climbs an eroded slope of earth and stones at **Morrete**, riven by small gullies and bearing a few small cairns. Climb past aulaga, tabaibal and verode on old, crumbling terraces, with prickly pears at a higher level. If the path is lost, avoid any thick scrub and walk on as much bare ground as possible, looking around to spot a **ruin**, at around 370m (1215ft), to get back on course.

From the ruin, the skyline looks like a heap of boulders. Aim to the right of it and a track will be joined, rising past tall yellow umbellifers called *cañalejas*. Cross a crest between small fields of black ash and follow the undulating track across a verdant slope of thick scrub and old terraces. A signposted junction is reached near a couple of palm trees at **Peña de la Pequeña**, at 459m (1506ft). Follow the track straight ahead, crossing a dip on the crest where there is a field of black ash and a building. The track rises gradually, passing more ash fields before suddenly turning right. At this point, spot a marker post on the left, where the route runs parallel to a road. ▶ The vegetation alongside might be tangled, but if tempted to walk along the road, bear in mind it is dead straight and the traffic goes fast. Pass stout walls that mark the **municipal boundary** between Haría and Teguise, around 540m (1770ft).

Watch for marker posts crossing the road and follow a track running parallel. Take the second track heading right, as marked, and follow it up between ash fields, passing a shelter and a small block ruin. There are a number of junctions; turn left to climb and reach a white building and a signpost beside a road. This stands at 596m (1955ft) on the slopes of **Peñas del Chache**, and is as close as the route gets to the highest point on Lanzarote, crowned with a radome and a military installation. ▶

Turn left to follow the road gently down to a junction on a broad gap, then follow a road up to the white **Ermita de las Nieves**, which is surrounded by palm trees on a broad hilltop at 594m (1949ft). It is worth leaving the road to look over a spectacular cliff to Caleta de Famara. Clearly, there are no direct descents. A mapboard and

This road can be followed to the right to the Restaurante Los Helechos, 1km (½ mile) away.

The surrounding area is surprisingly well-cultivated, watered by mist and dew.

Looking towards the radome on Peñas del Chache from a cliff edge near the Ermita de las Nieves

signpost stand beside the broad dirt car park at the ermita, and views stretch through the mountainous middle of Lanzarote to the neighbouring islands of Lobos and Fuerteventura.

Follow a broad dirt road downhill, flanked by white-painted stones as far as an enclosed military installation with an array of antennae. Continue down the dirt road, passing a signpost at **Cueva Bermeja**, at 461m (1512ft) on the way down to another signpost at **Pico de Maramajo**, at 449m (1473ft). Turn right here, but don't follow either of the two obvious vehicle tracks heading gently uphill.

Instead, look carefully to spot a marker post overlooking a steep slope, and only then turn left to follow a vague, stony, rocky path across a slope overlooking a deep, rugged barranco.

The path descends to a gap, keeping right of a square field of black ash and passing another marker post. ▶ Join a track and fork right uphill as marked, enjoying fine views back to the cliffs. Cross a little top and walk down to a broad, gravelly gap and a signpost at **Morro Alto**, at 325m (1065ft). Turn sharp right to pick up and follow a narrow path, descending at an easy gradient despite being on a steep, stony slope dotted with tabaibal, verode and lavender. The path gradually makes its way into the deep and rugged **Barranco de Maramajo**, crossing its bed around 160m (525ft). Scramble a short way up a stony slope and then follow the path downhill as it drifts away from the barranco through low scrub. Later follow a sandy streambed, crossing a little dam buried in sand and stones.

Reach a dirt road and turn right towards the **Urbanización Famara** – a housing development of bunker-like buildings. Turn left down a tarmac road, noting that there is a bar restaurant in the middle of the complex. The road has big aulaga bushes alongside it and

The island of La Graciosa and its neighbours come into view here.

Walks 10, 11 and 12 also finish here.

leads to sand dunes. Turn left to reach a road junction and then turn right to walk to **Caleta de Famara**, reaching a bus shelter. There are bar restaurants and shops, and the place is popular with surfers. ◀

WALK 16
Ye and Salinas del Río

Start/Finish	Las Rositas, near Ye
Distance	8km (5 miles)
Total Ascent/Descent	380m (1245ft)
Time	3hrs
Terrain	A steep descent on loose stones needs care, then easy paths lead to the coast. Reversing the route involves climbing the steep, stony path.
Refreshment	Bar restaurant at Ye.
Transport	Buses serving Ye are of no use to walkers. If arriving by taxi, ask to be dropped at Las Rositas.

A zigzag path breaches the dramatic cliffs of Risco de Famara, allowing walkers to get from the cliff-tops to the coast. An old salina (salt-pan) can be visited, and this is as close as walkers can get to the island of La Graciosa without actually going there. The hard part is climbing back to the top of the cliffs afterwards!

Only one bus a day reaches **Ye**, so late in the evening that this walk would have to start in the dark. If arriving by car or taxi, continue to **Las Rositas** and watch for the house called **Finca La Corona** on the right. Immediately after that, on the left, a stone-paved road leads to a car park. If coming from the **Mirador del Río**, along a splendid cliff-top road, this is the first place that cars can turn right. The car park stands around 360m (1180ft) and a stone-paved path heads towards the cliffs of **Risco de Famara**. A small viewpoint is reached beside a pylon, where you can look down a steep slope and winding path and decide

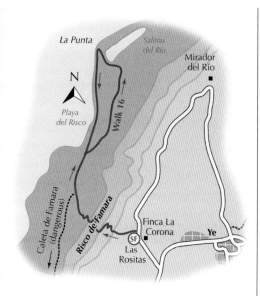

whether you really want to go down, knowing that you have to climb back!

The path is quite convoluted and starts with stone steps. Be careful all the way down: the stones covering the path are loose and it is unwise to hurry. An obvious pylon line also runs downhill, and the path zigzags to and fro, passing two pylons fairly close together and then passing another after a longer gap. Continue down a gentler, scrub-covered slope to reach a path junction and a cairn.

Turn right to follow an easy, gritty path, soon reaching a junction. ▶ Keep right, and soon afterwards cross a little ravine spanned by a pipeline. Keep right at another path junction and simply follow the path as it rises and falls gently, passing close to a ruin overlooking the **Salinas del Río**. Walk past the left-hand side of rectangular pools to reach a cobbly beach at **La Punta**. It is only 1km (½ mile) across the strait of El Río to the island of La Graciosa.

Head left to reach the sandy beach of Playa del Risco.

The Salinas del Río lie at the foot of the cliffs in this view from La Graciosa

Retrace steps to Las Rositas, maybe hugging the coast past **Playa del Risco** first. Bear in mind that the climb will doubtless be made in the hotter part of the day.

> Most walkers will hear about a spectacular path **traversing the Risco de Famara to Caleta de Famara**; it suffers regular rockfalls and landslides and is cut by crumbling gullies. When last inspected, places were noted where a slip would result in death. As the path is unlikely ever to be repaired, it can only get worse and cannot be recommended.

ISLA LA GRACIOSA

The strangely patterned slopes of the Agujas Grandes rise in the centre of the Isla La Graciosa

La Graciosa is frequently visited by day-trippers on the ferries from Orzola, but it is well worth staying on the island for at least a couple of nights and exploring it thoroughly on foot. If planning to camp, note that a permit has to be arranged in advance to use the basic campsite.

The Parque Natural del Archipiélago Chinijo has La Graciosa at its centre and also includes the smaller islands of Alegranza and Montaña Clara, the islets of Roque del Infierno and Roque del Este, as well as Lanzarote's awesome cliffs of Risco de Famara, which stretch from Orzola to Caleta de Famara. The smaller islands cannot normally be visited, but La Graciosa has excellent access and superb walking routes.

Walk 17 leaves Caleta del Sebo's sandy streets to climb Montaña del Mojón and Montaña Amarilla, returning across splendid sandy beaches. Walk 18 leaves Caleta del Sebo along a coastal path to reach the tiny settlement of Pedro Barba, later climbing Montaña Bermeja, with an option to visit the sandy beach of Playa de los Conchas.

WALK 17
Caleta del Sebo and Montaña Amarilla

Start/Finish	Caleta del Sebo
Distance	16km (10 miles)
Total Ascent/Descent	410m (1345ft)
Time	5hrs
Terrain	Mostly easy tracks, but also short, steep, stony and exposed paths on Montaña del Mojón and Montaña Amarilla.
Refreshment	Bar restaurants at Caleta del Sebo.
Transport	Occasional daily buses serve Orzola from Arrecife, Teguise and Punta Mujeres. Regular daily ferries link Orzola with Caleta del Sebo.

The southern and western half of La Graciosa is dominated by two small volcanoes. Montaña del Mojón is rarely climbed, despite having a good path around its crater rim, while Montaña Amarilla is popular but has steep and exposed slopes. Sandy beaches are crossed on the easy coastal walk back to Caleta del Sebo.

Step ashore at **Caleta del Sebo** and head left to the Restaurante Girasol. Walk straight inland along Calle La Popa and turn left along Calle Las Sirenas. Pass a burger bar and Las Pardelas apartments, then turn right along Calle Estribor to reach the edge of the village. Turn left and quickly right to follow a sandy track up a sandy, scrubby slope. The track features numbered disks, and a **farm** is passed at number 029. Continue up to a junction at number 069 and turn right along a narrower sandy track at **Peña Laja**. ◄

Keeping straight ahead, omitting Montaña del Mojón, saves 3km (2 miles) and 140m (460ft) of ascent/descent.

The path climbs a sandy, scrubby slope and passes a cairn shelter on a crest. It then heads for a prominent breach in the wall of a crater, where the ground becomes stony. Keep left and follow a short, steep, rugged path onto the rim of the crater. Another cairn shelter is reached on the 189m (620ft) summit of **Montaña del Mojón**. Enjoy the

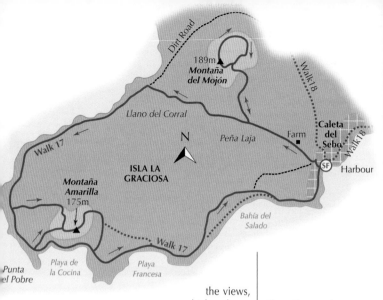

the views,
which embrace
La Graciosa and its neigh-
bouring islands, as well as the cliffs of Risco de Famara
on Lanzarote. A surprisingly good path makes a circuit

*The path around
Montaña del Mojón,
looking towards the
Agujas Grandes*

The village of Caleta del Sebo faces the dark cliffs of Risco de Famara

round the crater rim, but is rockier where it crosses a gap and then climbs to a lower summit at 178m (584ft). There are lots of cairns, then the path drops steeply and stonily, and steps are retraced to the track at disk number 069.

Continue along the track, crossing a broad and gentle gap while passing disk number 089. The track is worn and gullied as it descends to lower ground at **Llano del Corral** and joins a vehicle track. Turn left along the track, undulating gently, often with views of waves beating the rocky coast. Cross a series of stone-paved fords in streambeds that are usually dry, eventually reaching a turning space on low cliffs at **Punta del Pobre**. This lies at the foot of steep, rocky slopes on Montaña Amarilla, where there are three options for continuing, depending on the tide, or confidence on steep, rocky slopes.

For the safest ascent of the volcano, retrace steps from the turning space along the vehicle track, crossing three stone-paved fords. Next, turn right and climb a gentle, stony slope, avoiding gullies. The ground steepens and a crest is reached, where turning right and climbing steeply links with a path. Although steep and stony, requiring care, the gradients ease on the rim of the crater.

Even so, while following the crater rim past cairns and a trig point at 175m (574ft) on **Montaña Amarilla**, **care must be taken** where slopes drop steeply on both sides.

he path around the volcano's ridge later descends to the right; by keeping right at other path junctions the sandy beach of **Playa del Cocina** can be reached, while by keeping left it is possible to short-cut to the sandy beach of **Playa Francesa**.

Direct ascent of Montaña Amarilla

▶ Walkers who are confident scramblers can attempt a direct ascent, following a trodden path from the turning space past a lower hump, then carefully picking a way up steep, bare, yellow rock, to reach the darker rock above on the crater rim. Continue, still with care, to cairns and a trig point at 175m (574ft) on **Montaña Amarilla**.

Dangers include slipping and falling down steep rock slopes or falling into the sea.

Descend to the right from the volcano's ridge, and then either keep right at path junctions to reach **Playa del Cocina**, or keep left to short-cut to **Playa Francesa**.

Low tide option, avoiding ascent of Montaña Amarilla

▶ If the tide is out and the sea is calm, it is possible to scramble down the cliff from a 'rockfall' notice at the turning space. Cross a beach made of big rounded boulders; if this is completely free of water it is possible to follow a remarkable notch cut into the base of the mountain all the way to the sandy beach of **Playa de la Cocina**, where the main route can be rejoined and followed to **Playa Francesa**.

Dangers include slippery seaweed on the rock, 'freak' waves, and rockfall from above.

If you stay close to the coast, a sandy path links with a sandy track, which runs round a shallow tidal lagoon at **Bahía del Salado**. Continuing to follow the coast will lead you back into **Caleta del Sebo** along Avenida Virgen del Mar.

WALK 18
Caleta del Sebo and Montaña Bermeja

Start/Finish	Caleta del Sebo
Distance	19km (12 miles)
Total Ascent/Descent	250m (820ft)
Time	6hrs
Terrain	Easy coastal paths and inland tracks, with one steep and stony ascent and descent.
Refreshment	Bar restaurants at Caleta del Sebo.
Transport	Occasional daily buses serve Orzola from Arrecife, Teguise and Punta Mujeres. Regular daily ferries link Orzola with Caleta del Sebo.

The east and north of La Graciosa has a good coastal path, leading to a chasm and natural rock bridges at Los Arcos. The rugged little volcano of Montaña Bermeja can be climbed, and there is a fine sandy beach at its foot. A clear vehicle track allows for a rapid return across the middle of the island to Caleta del Sebo.

Step ashore at **Caleta del Sebo** and head to the right of the harbour, following any sandy streets parallel to the coast. When the edge of the village is reached, a path continues, flanked by parallel lines of stones and passing a solitary house. The ground features stones, sand and low scrub, and numbered disks are apparent. When number 103 is reached, an old track is followed as far as 184. A soft and sandy stretch runs from number 306 to 331, then an old limekiln is passed. Continue across a sandy slope and then cross a rocky slope with big boulders. An easy path continues from number 352 to **Pedro Barba**. ◄

A dirt road continues, but don't follow it. Instead, look for a narrow coastal path where black rocks have been pushed aside to reveal sandstone underneath. The path passes a trig point at **Punta de la Sonda**, at only 11m

This little settlement has odd-looking houses, palm trees, cacti and an arrangement of breakwater walls.

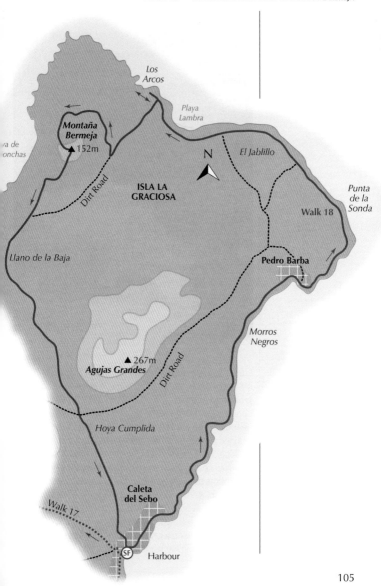

One of four fragile rock arches at Los Arcos, with the island of Alegranza in the distance

(36ft). Pass a metal notice and posts with a chain stretched between them, and follow a track across the sandy **El Jablillo** to another pair of chained posts. Pass these and continue walking gently up and around the big, sandy beach of **Playa Lambra**, reaching yet another pair of chained posts. The route heads inland, but first it is worth walking a little further along the coast to **Los Arcos**, where a narrow chasm is spanned by four flimsy rock bridges.

Follow the vehicle track inland, climbing gradually to a junction. ◀ Turn sharp right and follow a track towards the coast, but as it passes the open crater of a volcano, rising on the left, watch carefully to spot a vague path climbing up the crater rim. This becomes steep and stony as it climbs, quickly leading to the 152m (499ft) summit

A short-cut is available simply by walking straight ahead.

Walkers descending the crunchy red slopes of Montaña Bermeja

of **Montaña Bermeja**. Enjoy splendid views around La Graciosa, from the middle to the north of Lanzarote, then around the small islands of Roque del Este, Alegranza, Roque del Infierno and Montaña Clara. There might be carved rock sculptures on the summit.

Walk down a slope of loose, crunchy, red pumice and turn right at a path junction on the lower slopes to reach a car park. ▶ Follow the vehicle track onwards, keeping straight ahead at a junction, and later swing gradually left and climb gently to a broad gap in the middle of the island. There is a signposted track junction here, with a few cultivated plots in view. Simply walk straight ahead, over a very gentle crest around 50m (165ft) and descend to **Caleta del Sebo**.

The sandy beach of Playa de los Conchas is nearby.

107

GR 131 – PLAYA BLANCA TO ORZOLA

The GR 131 above the Iglesia de la Candelaria, with Montaña Blanca above (Walk 20)

The GR 131 is a long-distance trail traversing all seven of the Canary Islands and taking about a month to complete. A 72km (45 mile) stretch spans Lanzarote, and even those who are new to long-distance walking would find it easy to accomplish in five easy stages. There is no need to carry more than a day pack, as the route is well-served by buses, enabling walkers to 'commute' to and from each stage. Leaving Playa Blanca, a stone-strewn slope rises to Las Breñas, then an easy track continues to Yaiza.

After leaving Uga the route enters part of the wine-growing region of La Geria, then links a series of villages at the feet of old volcanoes on the way to San Bartolomé. After a gentle walk through the middle of the island to Teguise, it climbs close to the highest point on Lanzarote at Peñas del Chache, and then, after descending to Haría and passing through the neighbouring village of Maguéz, it climbs round the slopes of Monte Corona. The final stretch through the Malpais de la Corona leads to Orzola.

WALK 19
GR 131 – Playa Blanca to Yaiza

Start	Avenida Maritima, Playa Blanca
Finish	Antigua Escuela, Yaiza
Distance	15km (9½ miles)
Total Ascent	300m (985ft)
Total Descent	120m (395ft)
Time	5hrs
Terrain	Easy roads and tracks, then awkward, stony slopes to Las Breñas. Easy roads, tracks and paths to Yaiza.
Refreshment	Plenty of choice in Playa Blanca. Two bar restaurants in Las Breñas. Plenty of choice at Yaiza.
Transport	Regular daily buses link Playa Blanca and Yaiza with Arrecife. Limited services to Las Breñas are of little use.

The GR 131 leaves the sprawling resort of Playa Blanca and gradually rises across an extensive, old, broken lava flow to the village of Las Breñas. The route descends gradually, with views of extensive lava flows leading the eye to the Parque Nacional de Timanfaya. A track leads easily to the village of Yaiza.

Start at the small sandy beach in **Playa Blanca**, easily reached from the Avenida Marítima. Walk straight inland up Calle El Varadero, reaching a roundabout. The bus station lies left, but turn right to follow a pavement and cycleway, passing roadside strips planted with palm trees, cacti and aloe vera. The surroundings are a bit shoddy later, then buildings end on the edge of town. Turn left along an ash track, passing mounds of rubble dumped beside a housing development at **Hoya de la Yegua**. Turn left round a corner of a concrete wall, then turn right past more rubble, walking away from the development. Cross a track at **El Llano** and then keep right at a fork. The track leads to a wall and runs beside it, and the white **Casas del Terminillo** are seen.

A clear track crosses the foot of barren mountains, linking the villages of Las Breñas and Yaiza

When the wall turns right at a corner, veer left instead, crossing the access road that serves the buildings. A vague track runs roughly north a short way. Watch carefully for the continuation of a vague path; this was marked with small cairns and small blobs of blue paint, and should be improved as part of the GR 131. The path offers the only easy route across an extensive, broken lava flow covered in ankle-twisting stones. Eventually, white houses are seen perched on a brow ahead, and by the time a tumbled wall is reached, the path is clearer and easier to follow. Join a track and turn left to follow it, passing goat enclosures before a short, steep climb to a tarmac road on the outskirts of **Las Breñas**, over 100m (330ft). ◀

Notice how many houses have cactus gardens.

Turn right at a triangular road junction and follow Calle Los Roques. Turn left at the next junction, down Calle Victor Fernandez Gopar. The next junction features a bus shelter, where a right turn is made. Follow the road to yet another junction and turn left, passing below the attractive, terraced, shaded Plaza San Luis. ◀ Reach a complex road junction with roundabouts, a bus shelter

There is a bar restaurant above, opposite the church.

and access to a bar restaurant. Veer right along Calle La Cancela, following a quiet dual carriageway with palm trees along its centre. This road rises from the village, but suddenly bends sharp right to return to it. Leave the bend to continue straight along a track flanked by drystone walls, around 140m (460ft).

The track leads to a block-walled enclosure, where a path continues, descending gently across stony slopes bearing traces of old walls and enclosures.

The hills nearby, **Los Ajaches**, are significantly older than the red volcanic hills and rugged, black lava flows seen ahead, where the entire landscape dates only from the 1730s. Pale, stone-strewn slopes beside the path are almost barren, though occasional prickly pears flourish.

The path broadens and becomes a track running parallel to a road, while the road runs along the edge of a rugged black lava flow. The track crosses a paved dip then rises, passing a white house and olive terraces at the foot of **Montaña de la Cinta**. Continue along an embankment overlooking a large and attractive roundabout.

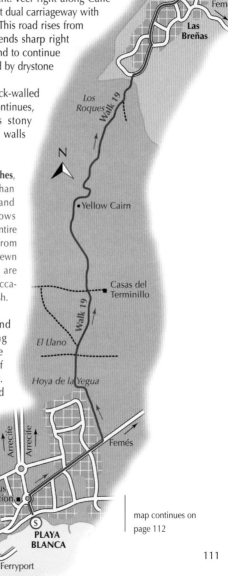

Femés

Las Breñas

Los Roques

Walk 19

N

• Yellow Cairn

Casas del Terminillo

Walk 19

El Llano

Hoya de la Yegua

Arrecife

Arrecife

Femés

Bus Station

S

PLAYA BLANCA

Ferryport

map continues on page 112

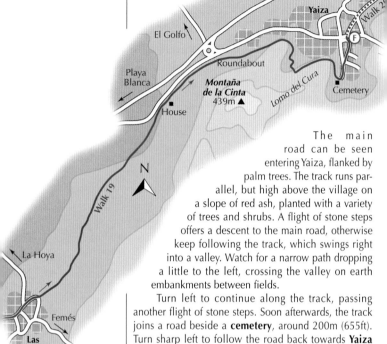

The main road can be seen entering Yaiza, flanked by palm trees. The track runs parallel, but high above the village on a slope of red ash, planted with a variety of trees and shrubs. A flight of stone steps offers a descent to the main road, otherwise keep following the track, which swings right into a valley. Watch for a narrow path dropping a little to the left, crossing the valley on earth embankments between fields.

Turn left to continue along the track, passing another flight of stone steps. Soon afterwards, the track joins a road beside a **cemetery**, around 200m (655ft). Turn sharp left to follow the road back towards **Yaiza** and walk down a road signposted 'La Era', between a play park and a large plaza. When a school is reached, keep to the right-hand side of the road to avoid being drawn through a tunnel, then turn right along the main road in the village to reach a junction beside the Antigua Escuela. ◂

The village has bar restaurants, shops, a bank, arts, crafts and bus services.

WALK 20

GR 131 – Yaiza to Montaña Blanca

Start	Antigua Escuaela, Yaiza
Finish	Tasca Mi Garaje, Montaña Blanca
Distance	16km (10 miles)
Total Ascent	480m (1575ft)
Total Descent	390m (1280ft)
Time	5hrs
Terrain	Roads and dirt roads, with occasional paths.
Refreshment	Bar restaurants at Uga. Small bars at Conil and Montaña Blanca.
Transport	Regular daily buses serve Yaiza, Uga, Conil and Montaña Blanca from Arrecife. Occasional weekday buses serve La Asomada from Arrecife

The trail between Yaiza and Uga is used in the morning and afternoon by hundreds of camels. Beyond Uga the wine-growing region of La Geria is covered in black volcanic ash. The route links the villages of La Asomada and Conil, before crossing a gap between two mountains to reach the village of Montaña Blanca.

Start at the Antigua Escuela, at a road junction in **Yaiza**, around 180m (590ft). Follow the road signposted for Tinajo and Timanfaya, going gently downhill and through a crossroads, then gently up past La Bodega de Santiago, where people drink and eat under an enormous tree. Follow the road past a roundabout and under a road bridge, then turn right at another roundabout as signposted. A road leads to a nearby house, but turn left beforehand along a track, passing an information board detailing volcanic eruptions of the 1730s. Soon afterwards, fork left along a path through a groove in a chaotic, blocky lava flow. The path surface is camel dung, as hundreds of camels walk this way, to and from the national park. Should you meet them, it may be wise to clamber onto the lava and let them pass!

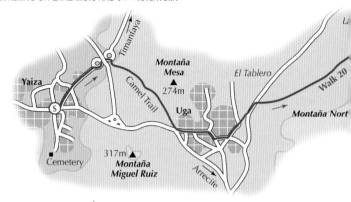

The village sits in a hollow, surrounding a deep pit where rainwater could be stored.

Pass another information board and follow an ash track that rises gently. Former vine pits lie to the left on the slopes of Montaña Meso, and level ash fields lie to the right. When the track reaches a road, turn left downhill and go straight through a crossroads, levelling out in the middle of **Uga**, at 214m (702ft). There are two bar restaurants, a supermarket, a church and bus services. ◀ Walk straight through the village, reaching a road junction on a bend where there is a play park. Turn left and follow the road, which immediately bends right, up to a crossroads. Turn left as marked, pass the last houses, then turn right and follow an ash track up to another road. Turn left along the road, then right where signposts and an information board stand at **El Tablero**, at 243m (797ft).

Follow an ash track up past a few ash fields; as it levels out and descends slightly the black ash landscape of **La Geria** stretches in all directions.

Thousands of pits have been dug into the ash, mostly with the addition of semi-circular drystone windbreaks, sheltering vines and occasional fig trees.

Follow the track ahead and gently uphill, avoiding tracks to left and right. The gradient steepens, with the ash wearing thin to expose older, lighter-coloured bedrock beneath. Signposts are passed as the track crosses

Montaña de
Guardilama
▲603m

Walk 7

La Montañeta

ña
ria

Walk 7

a broad gap, at 419m (1375ft), still among vineyards. Gentle **Montaña Tinasoria** rises to the right, with steep-sided **Montaña de Guardilama** to the left. ▶

Follow the dirt road steeply downhill on slopes of scrub with less cultivated areas in view. Arrecife is visible in the distance. Keep

map continues on page 116

Either or both could be climbed as 'extras', using tracks and paths clearly in view. Guardilama offers exceptional views of Lanzarote and five other islands!

Kilometre markers flank the GR 131, and Km50 has Montaña de Guardilama rising beyond it

115

straight ahead at a junction in a dip, rising again to cross a slight gap beside the gentle slopes of **La Montañeta**. Descend gently; the dirt road becomes a tarmac road, Camino de Caldereta, going down into the straggly village of **La Asomada**, reaching a signposted road junction at 315m (1035ft). ◄ Turn left up the road to reach a small supermarket, then turn right as signposted along the Camino El Callao II.

There is a bus stop down to the right.

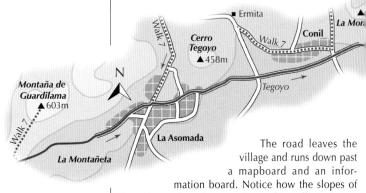

The road leaves the village and runs down past a mapboard and an information board. Notice how the slopes of **Cerro Tegoyo** have been engineered to collect rainwater, which is channelled into cisterns. Follow the road straight through the scattered hamlet of **Tegoyo** and then start climbing, gently at first, then more steeply to reach a crossroads around 280m (920ft). The GR 131 runs straight ahead, but it might be worth turning left for food and drink if a bar restaurant is open beside the church at **Conil**. ◄

Walk 7 also passes through the village.

Follow the road as it rises a little, passing a mapboard at a junction. Looking ahead, three hills stand in line, the furthest and palest being Montaña Blanca. The tarmac road, Camino Peña del Asiento, gives way to a dirt road that undulates and descends gently, passing cultivated and abandoned fields. Tías and its sprawling suburbs fill the slopes below. When another tarmac road is reached, turn right along it, but quickly leave it by following the second dirt road on the left. ◄

The tarmac road, Camino Los Fajardos, can be used to descend to Tías for a range of services.

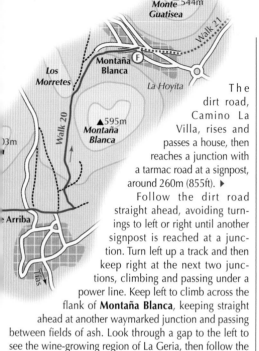

The
dirt road,
Camino La
Villa, rises and
passes a house, then
reaches a junction with
a tarmac road at a signpost,
around 260m (855ft). ▶

Follow the dirt road
straight ahead, avoiding turnings to left or right until another
signpost is reached at a junction. Turn left up a track and then
keep right at the next two junctions, climbing and passing under a
power line. Keep left to climb across the
flank of **Montaña Blanca**, keeping straight
ahead at another waymarked junction and passing
between fields of ash. Look through a gap to the left to
see the wine-growing region of La Geria, then follow the
track over a gap at 397m (1302ft). The village of **Montaña**

The church below,
Iglesia de la
Candelaria, has
a large plaza for
festivals and events.

*View from the lower
slopes of Montaña
Blanca, looking back
to the distant village
of La Asomada*

117

Blanca is seen below, with Monte Guatisea beyond. Step to the right of the track to follow a path down through a vegetated valley, passing a mapboard and information about the village. Follow a track onto a road, Calle Especiero, and continue down to a bus shelter and the little Tasca Mi Garaje bar, around 270m (885ft).

WALK 21
GR 131 – Montaña Blanca to Teguise

Start	Tasca Mi Garaje, Montaña Blanca
Finish	Church, Teguise
Distance	14.5km (9 miles)
Total Ascent	300m (985ft)
Total Descent	260m (855ft)
Time	4hrs 30min
Terrain	Easy roads and tracks, with an option to climb a steep mountain.
Refreshment	Small bar at Montaña Blanca. Plenty of choice at San Bartolomé and Teguise.
Transport	Regular daily buses serve Montaña Blanca, San Bartolomé and Teguise from Arrecife.

The first half of this stage is very convoluted, exploring the lower slopes of Monte Guatisea, between Montaña Blanca and San Bartolomé. It is possible to climb the mountain from the route. The route continues straight across a broad, gentle, sandy gap in the middle of Lanzarote to reach the former island capital of Teguise.

It is less than 1.5km (1 mile) by road to the centre of San Bartolomé, but the GR 131 takes a very convoluted route there.

Leave the little bar, Tasca Mi Garaje, in the lowest part of **Montaña Blanca**, and walk up Calle Lomo de Tesa, passing straight through a crossroads as signposted. Follow Calle San Bartolomé ahead and gently downhill, passing the last houses. Walk up a dirt road to pass an information board, then continue down the dirt road, almost joining a main road. ◄ Don't step onto the road, but keep left, passing the **Piensos y Forrajes** (feed and fodder) building, to follow another dirt road uphill. Pass little farms and cross a gap, around 330m (1085ft), to enter a cultivated hollow at **La Quinta**. ▶

Continue along the track, passing a junction with another track and later reaching a signposted junction with a rugged tarmac road. Turn right up the road, crossing a rise to enjoy views stretching beyond San Bartolomé. Just before entering the village, the

It is possible to climb Monte Guatisea from here – see Walk 8.

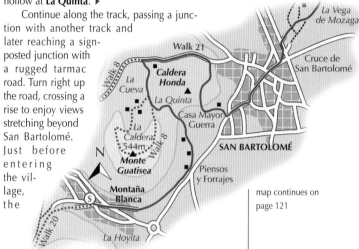

map continues on page 121

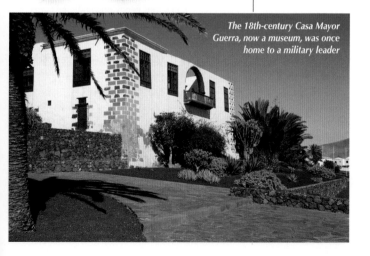

The 18th-century Casa Mayor Guerra, now a museum, was once home to a military leader

route turns right up another road, which quickly becomes a track passing a signpost. Cross a rise and continue downhill, turning left at a junction and crunching coarse ash underfoot. Follow a stone-paved path below the 18th-century **Casa Mayor Guerra**, and turn right down a broad stone-paved path to reach a road-end roundabout and an information board. ◄

This details the history of the house and its military former occupant.

Walk to the nearby main road and turn left to reach a mini-roundabout. Walk straight ahead as signposted for Tinajo and Teguise, along Calle Rubicón. Turn left at a roundabout bearing two palm trees, then right at a road junction, still following Calle Rubicón to the centre of **San Bartolomé**, around 260m (855ft). The fine Plaza Leon y Castillo rises to the left, and the interesting Museo Tanit is down to the right. ◄ Keep following Calle Rubicón, passing a mini-roundabout at a crossroads, then pass Finca Laconsura. Turn left along a short, brick-paved stretch of Calle Rubicón to reach a busy main road at **Cruce de San Bartolomé**.

The little town has a post office, banks, ATMs, bars, restaurants, shops, buses and taxis.

Turn left along the main road, use a pedestrian crossing at Pasteleria Lolita to cross to the other side, and then turn left again. Turn right along the quiet Calle Juan de Bethencourt, which runs gently downhill, the tarmac giving way to a dirt road that leaves town. Avoid a turning to a hilltop house and keep straight ahead at a junction

A dirt road leaves San Bartolomé and passes sandy fields on its way towards Teguise

of dirt roads to reach another junction at **La Vega de Mozaga**.

Fork right and pass between two little hills, or rock outcrops. Keep straight ahead through a dirt crossroads, passing sandy, stony fields while descending gradually to a broad dip at 180m (590ft). A rugged, broken lava flow lies ahead and the dirt road steps up onto it, becoming bendy. Pass a mast and reach a road junction.

Keep straight ahead, rising gently along a tarmac road, passing a little house and an ash field. Pass a white hut and another ash field, and follow the road up past more cultivated areas, keeping left at a junction to pass a **cemetery**. The road rises past more ash fields to reach a junction with a main road. Turn right towards a Cepsa filling station, but quickly turn left along another road. Turn right along Calle Pámpano, keeping left or straight ahead at a junction, then turn right at an 'ARTeguise' sign. Keep left again at the next junction and walk straight to the brick-paved Plaza Maciot

de Bethencourt. Keep straight ahead again through Clavijo y Fajardo, then turn right to reach the church of Nuestra Señora de Guadalupe in the centre of **Teguise**, around 300m (985ft). ▶

This was formerly the capital of Lanzarote; there is a full range of services, a Sunday market and plenty of fine, old buildings.

WALK 22

GR 131 – Teguise to Haría

Start	Church, Teguise
Finish	Plaza de la Constitución, Haría
Distance	14.5km (9 miles)
Total Ascent	360m (1180ft)
Total Descent	380m (1245ft)
Time	5hrs
Terrain	Dirt roads for most of the ascent, then a rugged cliff path. Tracks and stone-paved paths for the descent.
Refreshment	Plenty of choice at Teguise and Haría. Restaurant off-route at Los Helechos.
Transport	Regular daily buses serve Teguise and Haría from Arrecife.

The route leaves Teguise and heads towards the highest part of Lanzarote. Although the summit of Peñas del Chache is out of bounds, the trail picks its way along a dramatic cliff edge nearby. An old, winding, stone-paved path intersects a winding road on the way down to the delightfully interesting village of Haría.

Start at the church of Nuestra Señora de Guadalupe in the centre of **Teguise**, around 300m (985ft). Go behind it and walk straight across a huge paved plaza. Go up a flight of steps onto a road, Calle Puerto y Villa de Garachico, and turn right to follow it. When it approaches

map continues on page 124

N

Ermita de San José

Vega de San José

Football Ground

Ⓢ

TEGUISE

the edge of town, aim for a **football ground** and follow
a road past its far corner. The tarmac gives way to a dirt
road at a final housing block. Follow the dirt road ahead
and keep left at a fork. Next, avoid a track climbing
steeply to the left and keep walking ahead on the level.
Fork right at the next junction, cross a level area of fields
and earth pits, and pass the ruins of **Ermita de San José**.

Continue straight through a dirt crossroads and pass
a solitary little white building beside a field of black ash.
A broad path climbs a slope dotted with verode and
tabaibal, with bare rock and stone steps in places. Join a
dirt road at almost 400m (1315ft) and turn left to follow
it gently uphill along a broad, scrubby crest. The gently
rounded top of **Pico de Maramajo** is passed, where there
is a signpost at 449m (1473ft). ▶ Continue up the dirt
road and another signpost is passed at **Cueva Bermeja**, at
461m (1512ft). Pass an enclosed military installation with
an array of antennae. The dirt road is flanked by white-
painted stones as it climbs further, reaching a mapboard
and signposts beside a broad dirt car park. The white
Ermita de las Nieves is surrounded by palm trees, on a
broad hilltop at 594m (1949ft).

*Walkers following
a dirt road near
Teguise, which leads
towards the higher
parts of Lanzarote*

Walk 15 heads left,
and it is worth a short
detour here to look
over nearby cliffs.

map continues on
page 125

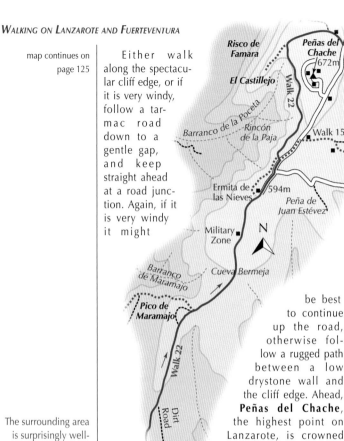

The surrounding area
is surprisingly well-
cultivated, watered
by mist and dew.

The summit of Peñas
del Chache is 674m
(2211ft).

Either walk along the spectacular cliff edge, or if it is very windy, follow a tarmac road down to a gentle gap, and keep straight ahead at a road junction. Again, if it is very windy it might be best to continue up the road, otherwise follow a rugged path between a low drystone wall and the cliff edge. Ahead, **Peñas del Chache**, the highest point on Lanzarote, is crowned with a radome and a military installation. ◄ Always stay near the cliff edge, over 600m (1970ft). Walk carefully and don't follow any paths over the edge. Eventually a track is joined and this quickly reaches a junction. Turn right to follow it past fields of scrub and black ash. Turning left leads along a crumbling, rocky crest to a remarkable viewpoint overlooking the cliffs of Risco de Famara.

Follow the track onwards, rising close to 630m (2065ft), which is the highest part of the route. ◄ Follow

A path picks its way across rugged slopes below the radome on Peñas del Chache

the track downhill, passing a goat farm before reaching a road and a signpost at **Llano de la Montaña**. Turn left to follow the road, then left again to follow a track, passing a couple of houses. ▶ Turn right down a stone-paved path on a slope bearing a wealth of plants, including tabaibal, verode, cañalejas and aeoniums. Cross a bendy road and continue down the path, soon crossing the road again. The next stretch of path passes below a road bend, and later crosses the road where a sign announces **Valle de Malpaso**.

A track descends above terraces of black ash, becoming a rugged path crossing the road yet again. Continue down a track, passing a big fig tree, to reach a signposted junction. Turn left and continue along the track, which runs onto a tarmac road. Pass the Casa/Museo César Manrique, which is worth visiting. From there it is simply a matter of following narrow streets into the centre of **Haría**, reaching a mapboard and signpost beside the Plaza de la Constitución, around 280m (920ft). If simply passing through the

The Restaurante Los Helechos lies 250m off-route by road.

125

The track descending towards
the village of Haría

village, follow the road signposted for Maguez; if leaving the route, turn right along a paved, pedestrianized, eucalyptus-shaded street to the church, where the bus stops are located. ▶

Haría has a bank with ATM, bars, restaurants, shops, bus services and taxis.

WALK 23
GR 131 – Haría to Orzola

Start	Plaza de la Constitución, Haría
Finish	Harbour, Orzola
Distance	12km (7½ miles)
Total Ascent	150m (490ft)
Total Descent	430m (1410ft)
Time	3hrs 30min
Terrain	Mostly easy roads and tracks, but more rugged towards the finish.
Refreshment	Plenty of choice at Haría. Bar restaurant at Máguez. Bar restaurant off-route at Ye. Bar restaurants at Orzola.
Transport	Daily buses serve Haría and Máguez from Arrecife, Teguise and Punta Mujeres. Daily buses serve Orzola from Arrecife, Teguise and Punta Mujeres.

A short road-walk links Haría and Maguez, then the GR 131 passes the steep slopes of Monte Corona. Wine-growing slopes give way to the rugged old lava flows of Malpais de la Corona – designated as a Monumento Natural. Rugged paths and tracks take the route through low-lying scrub to finish at the ferryport of Orzola.

Start in the centre of **Haría**, around 280m (920ft), on the Plaza de la Constitución, and take the road signposted uphill for Máguez. ▶ The road climbs to a complex junction on a gap, around 310m (1015ft). Simply follow the road down past the Bar Restaurante Los Cascajos, then turn left at a junction to continue into **Máguez**, around 260m (855ft). Walk straight through a crossroads, past a café bar, to follow the brick-paved Calle Santa Bárbara. Turn right at a crossroads along the curiously named street – A

If arriving by bus, walk from the church along a paved, pedestrianized, eucalyptus-shaded street, then turn right for Máguez.

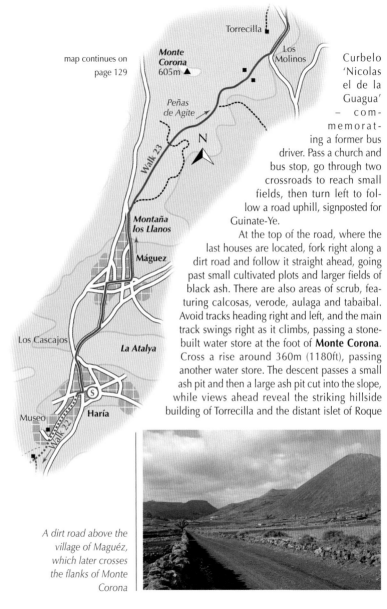

map continues on
page 129

Curbelo 'Nicolas el de la Guagua' – commemorating a former bus driver. Pass a church and bus stop, go through two crossroads to reach small fields, then turn left to follow a road uphill, signposted for Guinate-Ye.

At the top of the road, where the last houses are located, fork right along a dirt road and follow it straight ahead, going past small cultivated plots and larger fields of black ash. There are also areas of scrub, featuring calcosas, verode, aulaga and tabaibal. Avoid tracks heading right and left, and the main track swings right as it climbs, passing a stone-built water store at the foot of **Monte Corona**. Cross a rise around 360m (1180ft), passing another water store. The descent passes a small ash pit and then a large ash pit cut into the slope, while views ahead reveal the striking hillside building of Torrecilla and the distant islet of Roque

A dirt road above the village of Maguéz, which later crosses the flanks of Monte Corona

del Este. Calcosas, aulaga and lavender grow beside the track; then there are former vineyards, as well as areas planted with vines and almond trees.

Join a road at **Los Molinos** and follow it uphill until it turns left, around 330m (1080ft). ▶ Walk straight ahead from the road bend, down a dirt road. Rise and keep right at a junction at **Lajares**, then the dirt road turns right and runs downhill again. Pass old vineyards that mostly bear prickly pears, verode, aulaga and 'tobacco' trees. Pass a few houses at **Casas la Breña** and reach a road. Turn left to pass old lava flows that are green with lichen. Follow an ash path beside the road, as it later turns left to cross the lower slopes of **Lomo Blanco**. The path follows a wall and then makes a single zigzag down to fields planted with aloe vera. ▶

A track between fields leads to a narrow path among scrub. Pass through a hollow and follow a short stretch of stone-paved track. A dirt track leads to a track intersection, then another stone-paved stretch leads to a house. Afterwards, the track becomes a rugged riverbed, and one stretch runs through a deep, narrow cut. The bed broadens and is

Ye is 1km (½ mile) distant, with a bar restaurant.

A right turn leads to the Lanzaloe Shop.

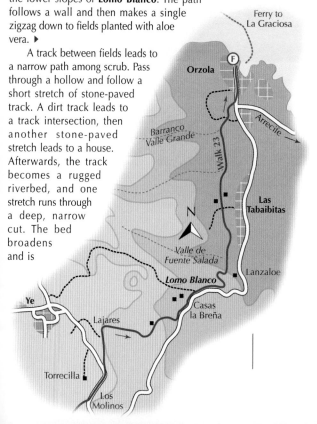

A winding track at Lajares, on the long descent towards Orzola

followed straight ahead, eventually reaching a road beside a bridge on the way into **Orzola**. Walk straight through the village, past a couple of shops and bar restaurants, to reach the harbour and the end of the GR 131. This is a busy place when ferries arrive and depart, and while the GR 131 doesn't visit the island of La Graciosa, walkers will find good walking there (see Walk 17 and Walk 18).

FUERTEVENTURA

A path runs across the lower slopes of
Montaña de Cardón (Walk 40)

INTRODUCTION

A long and very obvious track ascends gradually along a broad crest towards Pico de la Zarza (Walk 26)

Fuerteventura is the second-largest and the longest Canary Island. Many areas are used for agriculture, but struggle against desertification; other areas are rugged and stone-strewn. However, there are plenty of interesting walks and some routes have been improved in recent years. Over three weeks of walking are covered in this guidebook, split between day walks and a remarkable long-distance trail that stretches along the length of the island, taking nine days to complete.

The day walks on the island may be circular or linear, running from village to village, and there are usually good bus services for joining and leaving walks. The long-distance GR 131, however, has some stretches where buses are sparse or absent. Fuerteventura is renowned for its sandy beaches and dunes, and some fine examples are encountered on these walks. The island is sometimes whipped by strong winds, in which case sandy areas should be avoided. Due to the length of the island, it may be worth considering staying at a couple of bases to avoid spending long periods travelling to and from walks.

Map key

 Day walks

 Long-distance GR131

 Area boundary
Towns and villages
Roads

24
El Puer

Location of walks

Isla de Lobos

(45)

Corralejo

(35)

(44)

El Cotillo

(34)

Lajares

(36)

NORTH FUERTEVENTURA

La Oliva

(43)

Tindaya

(33)

Tefía

Tetir

(32)

(42)

Casillas del Ángel

PUERTO DEL ROSARIO

⊕ Airport

Betancuria

(31)

Antigua

(29)

(41)

Ajuy

(30)

Caleba de Fuste

Pájara

Tiscamanita

(40)

Tuineje

MID FUERTEVENTURA

(28)

Cardón

La Pared

Gran Tarajal

(39)

Costa Calma

NORTH ATLANTIC OCEAN

(27)

(38)

orro Jable

N

0   10 km

5 miles

There are about 355km (220 miles) of walking described on Fuerteventura in this book.

GETTING THERE

By Air
Flights to Fuerteventura from Gran Canaria and Tenerife are operated by Binter Canarias, tel. 902-391392, www.bintercanarias.com, and Canaryfly, tel. 902-808065, www.canaryfly.es. Buses offer links with Puerto del Rosario and the resorts of Caleta de Fuste, Gran Tarajal, Costa Calma and Morro Jable. Taxis are also available at the airport.

By Ferry
Two ferry companies operate regular services between Corralejo on Fuerteventura and Playa Blanca on Lanzarote: Lineas Fred Olsen, tel. 902-100107, www.fredolsen.es; and Naviera Armas, tel. 902-456500, www.naviera-armas.com. Less regular ferries link Morro Jable and Puerto del Rosario with Las Palmas on Gran Canaria.

GETTING AROUND

By Bus
Fuerteventura has good bus services from north to south, linking Corralejo, Puerto del Rosario and many towns and villages as far as Morro Jable. However, other places have less regular services, and timetables should be checked carefully with Tiadhe, tel. 928-855726, www.maxoratabus.com. The bus station does not supply printed timetables! Tickets are for single journeys and fares are paid on boarding the bus. Alternatively, buy a 'bono' card, load it with funds, and enjoy a 30% discount on fares. Buses are referred to as '*guaguas*', although bus stops, or *paradas*, may be marked as '*bus*'.

By Taxi
Long taxi rides are expensive, but short journeys are worth considering. The following numbers link with taxis around the island: Puerto del Rosario and Airport tel. 928-850216; Corralejo tel. 928-537441; Caleta de Fuste tel. 928-163004; Antigua and Betancuria tel. 928-878011; Gran Tarajal tel. 928-870059; Costa Calma tel. 928-541257; Morro Jable tel. 928-541257 (ask for the 4WD taxi if wanting to reach Cofete or El Puertito). Fares are fixed by the municipalities and can be inspected on demand, although negotiation might be possible.

ACCOMMODATION

Accommodation is abundant on Fuerteventura, although it is concentrated in the resorts of Corralejo, Caleta de Fuste, Gran Tarajal, Costa Calma and Morro Jable, as well as in the capital Puerto del Rosario. Elsewhere, small hotels and rural properties are widely spread. Many places that were once reserved for package tourists now cheerfully offer rooms and services to people who book at short notice or via the internet.

FOOD AND DRINK

Fuerteventura produces much of its own fruit, vegetables and fish. Some restaurants are cosmopolitan, while others offer good local fare. Specialities include goats' cheese. Wrinkly potatoes (*papas arrugadas*) cooked in salt are surprisingly refreshing in hot weather, served with hot *mojo roja* sauce or the gentler *mojo verde*. The fish used in most local fish dishes is *vieja*. If any dishes such as soups or stews need thickening, reach for the roasted flour *gofio*, which doubles as a breakfast cereal. Never pass up an opportunity to indulge in local fare!

TOURIST INFORMATION OFFICES

Puerto del Rosario tel. 928-850110
Airport tel. 928-860604
Caleta de Fuste tel. 928-163611
Corralejo tel. 928-866235
Ferryport tel. 928-537183
Gran Tarajal tel. 928-162723
Costa Calma tel. 928-875079
Morro Jable tel. 928-540776

The main tourism website for Fuerteventura is www.visitfuerte ventura.es

Camels once transported goods around the islands and now offer short rides for visiting tourists

JANDÍA

The lighthouse of Faro de Jandía at the extreme south-west end of the Punta de Jandía (Walk 37)

The long Jandía peninsula contains the highest mountain range on Fuerteventura, as well as extensive desert-like areas of sand and long, sandy beaches. Many visitors to the island stay on the peninsula, where popular resorts include Morro Jable and Costa Calma. The peninsula supports a good week's worth of walking. Walk 24 is a circular walk at the extreme western end of the peninsula, based on the tiny village of El Puertito. Walk 25 is a longer circular route crossing the mountain range between Morro Jable and Cofete. Walkers without vehicles should bear in mind that only one 4WD taxi will operate on the dirt roads west of Morro Jable.

Frequent bus services allow Walk 26 to be reached, and this route climbs to the highest point on Fuerteventura – Pico de la Zarza. Walk 27, around the shallow Laguna de Sotavento, is also well served by buses. The peninsula is so long that three days of the long-distance GR 131 (Walks 37 to 39) stretch along it, from El Puertito to Morro Jable and La Pared.

WALK 24

El Puertito and Las Talahijas

Start/Finish	El Puertito
Distance	12km (7½ miles)
Total Ascent/Descent	200m (655ft)
Time	4hrs
Terrain	Roads, tracks and sandy, stony paths through sparse scrub. Mostly gentle, but occasionally steep.
Refreshment	Bar restaurants at El Puertito
Transport	Ask for a 4WD taxi at Morro Jable. Normal taxis won't travel on the dirt road.

El Puertito is a ramshackle huddle of white houses at the end of the rugged Jandía peninsula, dominated by a single wind turbine. The village was founded by fishermen and offers a couple of little fish restaurants. The nearest hill is the barren, sandy, stony Las Talahijas, and this walk completely encircles it.

▶ Start at a junction of battered tarmac roads beside the village of **El Puertito**. A mapboard explains about the PR FV 56 to Caleta de Madera. Set off along a rather battered road, crossing a desert-like plain and rising gently. At one point the sea lies just to the left, at the foot of a crumbling cliff at **Playa de Ojos**. The road rises a little further, then there is a signpost on the right for Caleta de Madera. Follow a broad, sandy, gravelly track, often flanked by parallel lines of stones. Take care at a fork, keeping right along a gravelly track. As this rises a little more, yellow-and-white flashed marker posts are seen. Later, there is a steeper climb to almost 100m (330ft), on black rock, on the shoulder of **Las Talahijas**.

The track ends abruptly and a rugged path continues. This soon descends, as if aiming for the rock-walled **Caleta de la Madera**. At one point there is a view of two lighthouses – one on Punta de Jandía and the other on Punta Pesebre. The path, flanked by parallel lines of

Route uses PR FV 56 and GR 131.

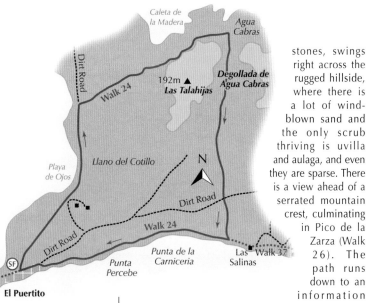

stones, swings right across the rugged hillside, where there is a lot of wind-blown sand and the only scrub thriving is uvilla and aulaga, and even they are sparse. There is a view ahead of a serrated mountain crest, culminating in Pico de la Zarza (Walk 26). The path runs down to an information board and signpost at **Agua Cabras**. Clumps of tamarisk bushes sit in a sandy valley. Turn right, walking uphill and inland along a sandy, gravelly track. ◄ Cross a broad gap between rugged hills, then follow a track down a slope bearing more tufts of scrub.

Note the beds of sand beside the track that are full of fossilised snail shells.

View around the cliffs of Caleta de la Madera towards Punta Pesebre

When a dirt road is reached there are two options: either turn right and follow the dirt road – which later becomes tarmac – back to the village, or cross the dirt road and follow a broad track towards the sea. The track runs to a beach at **Las Salinas**, but turn right beforehand when a white bollard is spotted. A short, steep, stony climb soon eases and a coastal path is marked with posts. These are flashed yellow, red and white, as the PR FV 56 runs concurrent with the GR 131 (Walk 37). The path follows low cliffs, such as **Punta de la Carniceria** and **Punta Percebe**, and passes little shingle and sandy beaches. Sometimes a huddle of houses can be seen ahead; if not, the prominent wind turbine is usually in view. ▶ When the wind turbine is reached, turn left to finish back at **El Puertito**.

Watch carefully for directional markers, avoiding any path marked with an 'X' or simply following the path closest to the sea whenever there is a choice.

WALK 25
Gran Valle and Cofete

Start/Finish	Gran Valle
Distance	25km (15½ miles)
Total Ascent/Descent	600m (1970ft)
Time	8hrs
Terrain	Easy valley path, followed by a rugged mountain pass. Easy dirt roads, with an option to join a more rugged path.
Refreshment	Bar restaurant at Cofete.
Transport	Ask for a 4WD taxi at Morro Jable. Normal taxis won't travel on the dirt road.

This long circuit takes in a big valley, a splendid mountain pass, a remote village with a bar restaurant, and an optional visit to an enormous sandy beach. Afterwards, either return the same way or follow a dirt road across another pass, possibly switching to a waymarked path back to the start.

▶ The start is about 3km (2 miles) west of the outskirts of Morro Jable. A dirt car park lies beside the road at **Gran**

Route uses PR FV 55 and GR 131.

map continues on
page 142

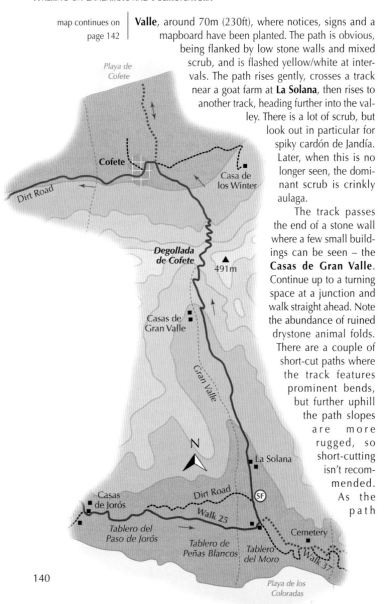

Valle, around 70m (230ft), where notices, signs and a mapboard have been planted. The path is obvious, being flanked by low stone walls and mixed scrub, and is flashed yellow/white at intervals. The path rises gently, crosses a track near a goat farm at **La Solana**, then rises to another track, heading further into the valley. There is a lot of scrub, but look out in particular for spiky cardón de Jandía. Later, when this is no longer seen, the dominant scrub is crinkly aulaga.

The track passes the end of a stone wall where a few small buildings can be seen – the **Casas de Gran Valle**. Continue up to a turning space at a junction and walk straight ahead. Note the abundance of ruined drystone animal folds. There are a couple of short-cut paths where the track features prominent bends, but further uphill the path slopes are more rugged, so short-cutting isn't recommended. As the path steepens, straggly 'tobacco' trees stabilise the rocky and stony slopes. Watch for a short path down to the left, which allows a cave to be visited, cut in search of groundwater. A final rugged climb leads to the **Degollada de Cofete**, at 343m (1125ft). Views stretch back through Gran Valle, taking in nearby mountains, while on the other side the village of Cofete is seen, as well as the big house of Casa de los Winter and a long, golden, sandy beach.

The path downhill is very good, despite cutting across a steep and rocky slope. Nearby mountains look impressive, and are seen from every angle as the path winds and zigzags. After passing a broad, gravelly space, the path descends gently, reaching a dirt road beside the first houses in the ramshackle village of **Cofete**, around 60m (195ft). Either walk straight ahead to follow the dirt road away from it, or explore first.

Walk down to a triangular junction of dirt roads and note the Restaurante Cofete up to the left. ▶ A mapboard and signpost stand at the junction, and it is another 1km (½ mile) to the beach. Turn right to follow the dirt road to

A restored limekiln has a sculpture of a man and dog on it.

The start of the narrow path that descends from the Degollada de Cofete to the village of Cofete

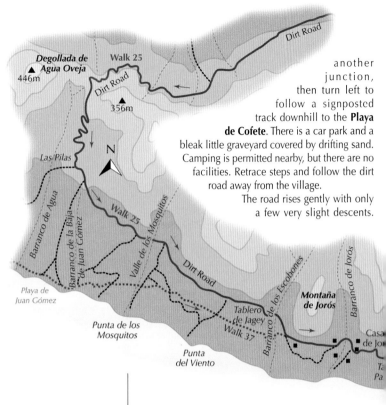

another junction, then turn left to follow a signposted track downhill to the **Playa de Cofete**. There is a car park and a bleak little graveyard covered by drifting sand. Camping is permitted nearby, but there are no facilities. Retrace steps and follow the dirt road away from the village.

The road rises gently with only a few very slight descents.

Masses of cardón grow among the scrub on the stony slopes. A junction is reached where a track descends to the coast at Roque del Moro, but walk straight ahead as signposted for Morro Jable. The cardón vanishes around here, and other scrub becomes very sparse on the rocky, stony slopes. The road continues towards a prominent pyramidal peak and crosses a gap, **Degollada de Agua Oveja**, at 230m (755ft). Enjoy views both ways and then descend. The road is exceptionally bendy, without short-cuts, but a junction is soon reached around 100m (330ft) at **Las Pilas**, where there are signs and notices.

Turn left for Morro Jable, but decide whether to stay on the dirt road or switch to a traffic-free path. The dirt

The course of the long-distance GR 131 can be followed back towards Gran Valle

road is obvious, falling and rising gently across rugged slopes. ▶ If the road is followed, watch the slopes alongside after passing a track signposted for Baja Gómez, near the **Valle de los Mosquitos**. Cardón de Jandía grows on both sides for a short while. Eventually the dirt road swings left into the rubble-strewn **Barranco de los Escobones**, where there is a ruined concrete building. The GR 131 joins from the right and follows the road a short way.

Turn left as signposted along a rugged path, which later drops directly to the road beside a white building. There are other buildings, former cultivated plots, a couple of palms, tamarisks and spurge-like trees at the **Casas de Jorós**. Turn left to follow the road round a

To use the path, take any of the next four tracks down to the right, turning left to follow the red-and-white flashed GR 131, as described in Walk 37.

143

bend, passing a mapboard. Follow the road away from the buildings, across stony slopes bearing little tufts of scrub. Watch for a GR 131 signpost on the right, where a clear path leaves the road. The path gradually drifts from the road, crossing tracks and dry streambeds. A group of buildings is approached, but before reaching them the path swings left and returns to the dirt road. Turn left to follow the road back to the car park at **Gran Valle**. ◄

Cross the road to follow the GR 131 to Morro Jable.

WALK 26
Pico de la Zarza

Start/Finish	Ventura Shopping Centre, Playa de Jandía
Distance	15.5km (9½ miles)
Total Ascent/Descent	890m (2920ft)
Time	5hrs 30min
Terrain	Urban, then a vehicle track climbs along a broad, stony, bouldery mountain crest. The final ascent is a rugged path with stone steps.
Refreshment	Plenty of choice around Playa de Jandía
Transport	Regular daily buses serve Playa de Jandía from Puerto del Rosario and most towns and villages in the middle of Fuerteventura.

This is the highest mountain on Fuerteventura, offering the longest continuous ascent on the island. The route starts at sea level and is mostly accomplished along a vehicle track, ending with a zigzag path on the bouldery upper slopes. Cloud permitting, there are excellent views of the Jandía peninsula.

Route uses PR FV 54.

◄ Either start from the **Ventura Shopping Centre**, or, if walking from one of the nearby resorts, follow the promenade until a mapboard and signpost are reached for the PR FV 54. Go through a subway beneath the main FV-2 road, then walk up a road to the right of the shopping centre. There are yellow/white flashes on road signs. Climb

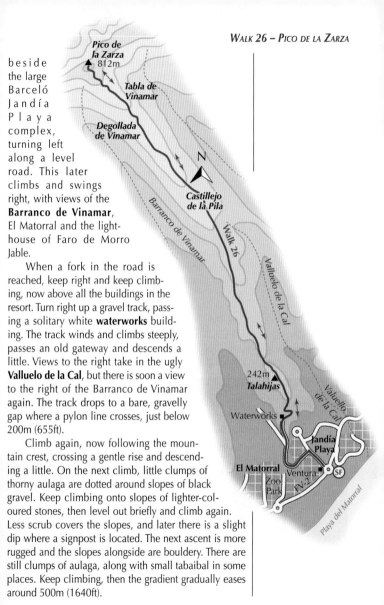

beside the large Barceló Jandía Playa complex, turning left along a level road. This later climbs and swings right, with views of the **Barranco de Vinamar**, El Matorral and the lighthouse of Faro de Morro Jable.

When a fork in the road is reached, keep right and keep climbing, now above all the buildings in the resort. Turn right up a gravel track, passing a solitary white **waterworks** building. The track winds and climbs steeply, passes an old gateway and descends a little. Views to the right take in the ugly **Valluelo de la Cal**, but there is soon a view to the right of the Barranco de Vinamar again. The track drops to a bare, gravelly gap where a pylon line crosses, just below 200m (655ft).

Climb again, now following the mountain crest, crossing a gentle rise and descending a little. On the next climb, little clumps of thorny aulaga are dotted around slopes of black gravel. Keep climbing onto slopes of lighter-coloured stones, then level out briefly and climb again. Less scrub covers the slopes, and later there is a slight dip where a signpost is located. The next ascent is more rugged and the slopes alongside are bouldery. There are still clumps of aulaga, along with small tabaibal in some places. Keep climbing, then the gradient gradually eases around 500m (1640ft).

The track descends gently and drifts away from the crest, so that it overlooks the Barranco de Vinamar. The track is grit and gravel, easy for walking, but the slopes alongside are covered in large boulders, blotchy with lichen.

> Tabaibal now dominates the scrub, and there are also asphodels, but later aulaga becomes dominant. Straggly 'tobacco' trees bind the slopes alongside.

Reach a gentle gap and climb again, with the surface becoming rough and stony. A broad area of gravel is reached at **Tabla de Vinamar**, where there is a signpost.

The vegetation beside the path has been chewed by goats and includes thorn bushes, verode and Canary Island daisies (*Astericus sericeus*). Pass a notice explaining how Fuerteventura was created; the path the narrows but remains obvious. Zigzag up a steep, bouldery slope, climbing chunky stone steps in places. Go through a gate into a fenced enclosure, noting the abundance of Canary Island daisies, which are safe from goats here. They provide a colourful display early in the year at the top of the mountain.

A signpost halfway along the route to the summit, below Castillejo de la Pila

There is a trig point on **Pico de la Zarza**, at 812m (2664ft), and an alarmingly abrupt cliff edge. Look down on the long beaches of Playa de Cofete and Playa de Barlovento, and spot the village of Cofete. Mountains either side of the summit are jagged and rocky; they look attractive but are difficult for ordinary walkers to traverse. After a suitable break, retrace steps all the way back down to **Jandía Playa**. The coastal resorts and landmark Faro de Jandía are in view almost all the way.

Pico de la Zarza – the highest point on Fuerteventura and the highest of all the summits in this book

WALK 27
Costa Calma and Playa de Sotavento

Start	Costa Calma
Finish	Hotel Meliá Gorriones
Distance	12km (7½ miles)
Total Ascent/Descent	30m (100ft)
Time	3hrs 30min
Terrain	Mostly sandy beaches, but some rocky ones too. Check that the tide will be out for the duration of the walk.
Refreshment	Beach bars at Costa Calma, Bahía Calma, Sotavento, Casas Risco del Paso and Gorriones.
Transport	Daily buses link Costa Calma with Morro Jable, Puerto del Rosario and all points in-between. Some buses detour to the Melia Gorriones.

The shallow tidal lagoon of Sotavento is protected from the deep Atlantic by a broad sand bar. At low water, a complete circuit can be made around it, while tidal channels are easily waded. It is well worth approaching the lagoon from the resort of Costa Calma, taking in a series of sandy and rocky beaches.

Start at the bus stop beside the roundabouts in the lowest part of **Costa Calma**. Face the Hotel Fuerteventura Playa

Passing a small cliff between the Playa de Costa Calma and Playa de Sotavento

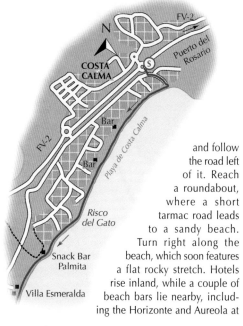

map continues on
page 150

and follow the road left of it. Reach a roundabout, where a short tarmac road leads to a sandy beach. Turn right along the beach, which soon features a flat rocky stretch. Hotels rise inland, while a couple of beach bars lie nearby, including the Horizonte and Aureola at

Wading is required where the shallow Laguna de Sotavento connects with the Atlantic Ocean

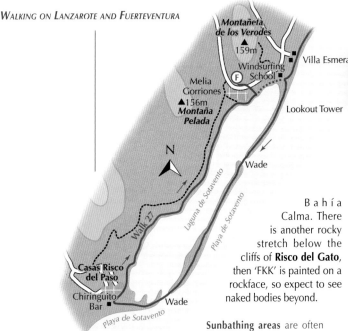

Bahía Calma. There is another rocky stretch below the cliffs of **Risco del Gato**, then 'FKK' is painted on a rockface, so expect to see naked bodies beyond.

Sunbathing areas are often divided into sectors and zones, where sun loungers can be hired.

Pass small caves and overhanging rock while crossing sandy, rocky and bouldery areas. Pass the **Snack Bar Palmita** to reach a sandy beach beyond. Pass beneath the **Villa Esmeralda** and cross another rocky patch to reach a **windsurfing school** and café, with palm trees alongside.

Confirm the state of the **tide** at the windsurfing school, and if an exit is needed, head for the Meliá Gorriones hotel.

A long sand bar ahead has deep sea to the left and the shallow **Laguna de Sotavento** to the right; the plan is to walk along the bar, noting that it can be breached at high water and should be avoided in stormy weather. In strong winds, bare flesh gets scoured by wind-blown sand.

Walk along the sand bar, aiming for the lifeguard's **lookout tower**. People may be seen walking through the lagoon, rarely knee-deep in water. Continue along the sand bar, and even at low water at least two shallow channels need to be waded. Simply keep walking until it is possible to walk straight to a building on the beach near the **Casas Risco del Paso**. This is the **Chiringuito Bar**, which has a sand floor and woven cane walls. ▶

The walk continues along the landward side of the lagoon, hugging the break of slope between the sandy shore and the rocky or sandy slopes rising inland. An incoming tide isn't a problem, since it is easy to stay out of the water. The tidal sands are dotted with succulent bushes that withstand saltwater. The route passes the feet of Risco del Paso, Morrete de los Castrillos and **Montaña Pelada**. Just as the **Meliá Gorriones** hotel is reached, a road heads inland. However, it is worth staying beside the lagoon a little longer, passing the 'Kite Center' and its café. A little further along, after passing private steps to the hotel, a sandy groove leads up to a road. The road leads to the front entrance of the hotel, where a bus stop stands opposite. ▶

A view of the shallow lagoon, narrow sandspit and extensive ocean from above the Chiringuito Bar

The GR 131 heads inland and can be followed to catch a bus. See Walk 38.

Alternatively, retrace steps back along the beach to Costa Calma, if the tide still allows.

151

MID-FUERTEVENTURA

Looking towards Montaña de Cardón from the crest of Morro de Moralito

The best walks in the middle of Fuerteventura are found in the mountains, and particularly where old mountain paths have been recently cleared, repaired, signposted and waymarked. Walkers without cars will find that areas away from the main roads are poorly served by bus. The little village of Cardón has a very limited bus service, but the splendid short Walk 28 is available onto Montaña de Cardón, a protected Monumento Natural. Walk 29 is almost entirely routed through a barranco, linking the mountain village of Vega de Río Palmas with the coastal village of Ajuy. Its highlights include the rocky Barranco de las Peñitas and a short coastal walk to the Arco del Jurado.

Plenty of buses serve Tiscamanita and Agua de Bueyes, where Walk 30 climbs easily over Morro Jorjada. Walk 31 offers an easy route over a mountain gap to link the villages of Antigua and Betancuria. Two splendid stages of the GR 131 also pass through this area, linking La Pared, Cardón, Pájara, Vega de Río Palmas and Betancuria.

WALK 28
Cardón and Montaña de Cardón

Start/Finish	Cardón
Alternative	
Start/Finish	Barranco de los Tanques
Distance	4 or 9.5km (2½ or 6 miles)
Total Ascent/Descent	150 or 210m (490 or 690ft)
Time	1hr 30min or 3hrs
Terrain	Easy road and tracks, then a path that is mostly easy but occasionally steep.
Refreshment	Bar and café at Cardón.
Transport	Limited bus service of little use to walkers.

The Monumento Natural Montaña de Cardón features rocky terraces and towers. The lower slopes of the mountain support cardón, from which it gets its name. This there-and-back walk visits an interesting spring of water high on the mountain at El Tanquito, where there is also a curious shrine in a cave.

▶ Start at a bus shelter and crossroads at **Cardón**. Follow the Camino de Vista Cabeza past a bar and church, signposted as the GR 131 to Pájara. Step down to the right later to continue along a dirt road in the bed of a barranco. Tarmac roads climb right and left, and one road climbing left is signposted for El Tanquito, where a mapboard highlights the SL FV 53 trail. Walk up the road, turning left at the first junction and right at the second, then cross a dip. The road winds up to a signpost, where a right turn leads along a short road. This undulates, passing little farms and cultivated plots. Either join a road and turn right to follow it up to a small **car park** then turn left down a path, or drop into a dry streambed and go through a **tunnel** beneath the road.

If the latter choice is made, exit the tunnel, climb to the left to follow a road onwards, then fork right along

Route uses GR 131 and SL FV 53.

Montaña Redonda ▲442m

Car Park

ASF

Montaña Hendida

Tunnel

Barranco de los Tanques

Walk 28

N

El Castillo ▲663m

El Tanquito

Montaña de Cardón ▲694m

Cardón

SF

Walk 40

a track. Follow this as far as a hut, then look carefully to spot a path on a nearby slope, marked by parallel lines of stones. Walk along the path, keeping left of the barranco bed and well above it, then cross a rubble dam to reach a signpost and turn left. ◀

A clear path crosses a streambed and climbs past a mapboard. It later zigzags up a steep and stony slope, where only a few bushes are dotted around. Walk along a rounded crest and drift left from a signpost, cutting across a slope to reach a broad gap marked by a tall pole. The path undulates across a steep, stony, bouldery slope, but is actually quite easy. Vegetation is limited to aulaga, verode and thorny bushes. Go through a gate and climb past a noticeboard. Ahead is a fine spring of water and a curious cave/ermita at **El Tanquito**.

The road and small car park are just up to the right.

A clear and obvious path climbs onto the shoulder of Montaña de Cardón

Although there is another gate and a narrow path continues, this crosses steep, crumbling slopes that are unsafe. Rather than attempt to climb **Montaña de Cardón**, retrace steps to the road, if parked there, or back to the village.

WALK 29
Vega de Río Palmas to Ajuy

Start	Vega de Río Palmas
Finish	Ajuy
Distance	13km (8 miles)
Total Ascent	100m (330ft)
Total Descent	350m (1150ft)
Time	4hrs
Terrain	Mostly easy paths, with a couple of rocky stretches.
Refreshment	Bar restaurants at Vega de Río Palmas and Ajuy.
Transport	Daily buses from Puerto del Rosario to Vega de Rio Palmas. Arrange a pick-up from Ajuy.

This easy walk follows a barranco from the mountains to the coast. The scenery is impressive at first, with lots of steep, bare rock. It is much gentler beyond, passing a hidden stream among palm trees. Once the coast is reached, a simple walk leads to an islet featuring the fine rock arch of Arco del Jurado.

▶ If the bus is used to reach **Vega de Río Palmas**, walk back from the final stop and down to a bridge, car park and signposts, at 240m (790ft). Walk through the car park, following a path through dense stands of cane, palms and tamarisk, where a trickle of water might be flowing through rock pools. Continue along a stony track in the bed of the **Barranco de las Peñitas**, enjoying views of surrounding mountains. When the track rises to the right, keep left, passing mixed scrub and an information board. ▶ The path has a rope fence alongside as it passes

Route uses SL FV 6.

This tells a local legend accounting for the building of a nearby ermita.

The Ermita de las Peñitas, on the way from Vega de Río Palmas to the Barranco de Mal Paso

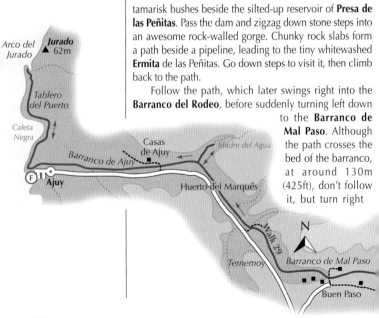

tamarisk bushes beside the silted-up reservoir of **Presa de las Peñitas**. Pass the dam and zigzag down stone steps into an awesome rock-walled gorge. Chunky rock slabs form a path beside a pipeline, leading to the tiny whitewashed **Ermita** de las Peñitas. Go down steps to visit it, then climb back to the path.

Follow the path, which later swings right into the **Barranco del Rodeo**, before suddenly turning left down to the **Barranco de Mal Paso**. Although the path crosses the bed of the barranco, at around 130m (425ft), don't follow it, but turn right

Easy walking along the dry, gravelly riverbed of the Barranco de Ajuy

a short way along the rugged bed to link with a stony track. ▶ Follow the track easily along the bed of the barranco, passing a handful of small farms.

The way ahead is always clear, although a couple of tracks cross over, serving little farms. The bed of the barranco bends to the right, then later bends to the left. At this point a little barranco to the right is filled with palm trees, and it is worth entering it a short way to see a small stream and the pool of water at **Madre del Agua**. Double back and continue along the broad bed of what is now the **Barranco de Ajuy**, often flanked by palm trees and tamarisk bushes. Walk all the way to a black sand beach; the village of **Ajuy** lies to the left and features a handful of bar restaurants.

The path across the barranco goes through an area of fenced plots containing regenerating palm trees.

It is worth exploring the coast on a short there-and-back walk. A stone-paved path with a fence alongside climbs from the beach onto rugged

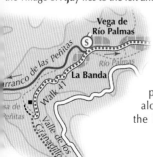

sandstone cliffs. The path runs along a terrace, reaching old limekilns. Keep right at a junction, as signposted for **Caleta Negra**. This rugged cove is reached by turning left at another junction and going down steps to enter a sea cave. There is no exit, so double back along the path, as if returning to Ajuy. However, as soon as the path begins to descend, turn sharp left up through a gap in a fence. Follow a trodden path, keeping clear of crumbling cliff edges, which rise over 40m (130ft) from the sea. The slopes are stony and bear a little aulaga and uvilla.

Cross a little ravine and go through a gap in another fence. Views ahead soon reveal a rocky islet connected to the mainland by a storm beach. Pick a way carefully down a rocky nose to reach the beach and walk to the islet. At closer quarters, the rock arch of **Arco del Jurado** can be seen. Retrace steps to Ajuy to finish.

WALK 30
Tiscamanita and Morro Jorjado

Start/Finish	Tiscamanita
Distance	13km (8 miles)
Total Ascent/Descent	500m (1640ft)
Time	4hrs
Terrain	Roads and dirt roads at the start and finish. Clear paths on the hills.
Refreshment	Bar restaurants at Tiscamanita.
Transport	Regular daily buses serve Tiscamanita and Agua de Bueyes from Puerto del Rosario and Morro Jable.

The village of Tiscamanita boasts a fine windmill that catches the eye of anyone passing on the main road. Less obvious is a path leaving the village, climbing onto Morro Jorjado. It is possible to descend to Vega de Río Palmas, or Agua de Bueyes. If the latter is chosen, a circuit can be completed back to Tiscamanita.

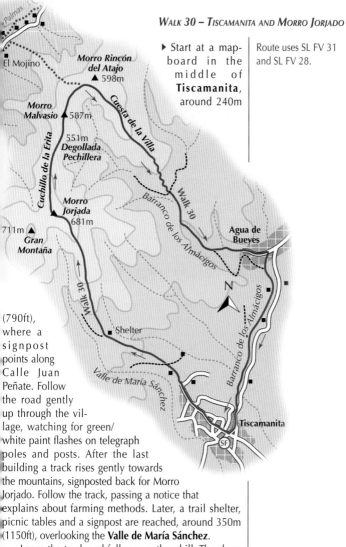

▶ Start at a map-board in the middle of **Tiscamanita**, around 240m

Route uses SL FV 31 and SL FV 28.

(790ft), where a signpost points along Calle Juan Peñate. Follow the road gently up through the village, watching for green/white paint flashes on telegraph poles and posts. After the last building a track rises gently towards the mountains, signposted back for Morro Jorjado. Follow the track, passing a notice that explains about farming methods. Later, a trail shelter, picnic tables and a signpost are reached, around 350m (1150ft), overlooking the **Valle de María Sánchez**.

Leave the track and follow a path uphill. The slope is stony and occasionally rocky, but the path is obvious. Climb past sparse scrub, noting prickly pears and aloes

159

An obvious path, flanked by parallel lines of stones, climbs steadily towards Morro Jorjado

later, with more vigorous scrub and bushes passed further uphill. The path almost gets onto a broad crest as it winds and climbs, passing lots of tabaibal and verode. The scrub thins on the stony top of **Morro Jorjado**, where a trig point is passed at 681m (2234ft). Enjoy a fine panorama, taking in nearby and distant ranges of hills, as well as the plains stretching beyond Tiscamanita, which are dotted with many other villages.

Follow an obvious path northwards, downhill and along a high crest, passing little stone windbreaks. Cross the broad gap of **Degollada Pechillera**, at 551m (1808ft). The path rises and crosses the rounded top of **Morro Malvasio**, at 587m (1926ft). Continue alongside a fence and down to a bare, stony gap and a signpost at

It is possible to descend left, 2km (1¼ miles) to Vega de Río Palmas, linking with the GR 131. See Walk 41.

569m (1867ft). ◄ Turn right to start descending to Agua de Bueyes. The path cuts across a slope featuring wonderfully mixed bushy scrub, passing a tiny shelter with a wooden cross on top. The descent is gentle and follows the stony crest of **Cuesta de la Villa**, with sparse scrub. Eventually, swing right from the crest; the path becomes more rugged, with more scrub alongside. Wind down to

a trail shelter, picnic tables, mapboard and signpost near a junction of dirt roads, around 330m (1080ft).

Walk straight ahead along a dirt road through the **Barranco de los Almácigos**, passing farms, cultivated plots and palm trees, reaching a mapboard and continuing along a tarmac road. Pass another mapboard and a church, then cross a dip in the road at **Agua de Bueyes**. ▶ Turn sharp right to follow a dirt road along the bed of a barranco, quickly joining another dirt road back in the **Barranco de los Almácigos**. The descent is very gentle and the way ahead is obvious, running parallel to the main road. Pass a few houses and fields surrounded by earth embankments. Eventually, the main road has to be followed, and it is best to cross it and rise into **Tiscamanita**, following a broad tarmac path. Either finish at one of the bus shelters, visit the windmill, or take a break at one of the bar restaurants.

After crossing Morro Malvasio, the route heads right for Agua de Bueyes.

Walk straight ahead to the main road and bus stops.

WALK 31
Antigua to Betancuria

Start	Calle General Franco, Antigua
Finish	Bus stop, Betancuria
Distance	6km (3¾ miles)
Total Ascent	350m (1150ft)
Total Descent	210m (690ft)
Time	2hrs
Terrain	Easy roads and tracks, with an easy path crossing a mountain gap.
Refreshment	Bar restaurants at Antigua and Betancuria.
Transport	Regular daily buses serve Antigua from Puerto del Rosario and Morro Jable. Occasional daily buses serve Betancuria from Puerto del Rosario.

Walkers without cars sometimes complain that they can't get to Betancuria in the mornings. This short walk makes it possible by starting early from Antigua, following a clear path and track over a gap in the hills. It's possible to arrive long before the tourists, and still have the rest of the day to explore and walk in the area.

Route uses SL FV 14.

◄ The village of **Antigua**, situated at around 250m (820ft), has a hostal, post office, bank with ATM, shops, bars, buses and taxis.

Walk south from the bus stops to spot a play park on the right, and turn right along Calle General Franco. There is a mapboard opposite a taxi stand, with a signpost for Betancuria. Walk steeply down Calle El Molino and climb past houses as the road levels out. A windmill, **Molino de Durazno**, stands to the right, but keep straight ahead as signposted down a road. ◄ Follow the road gently up past cultivated areas, but when it suddenly turns right, a signpost points ahead up a gently rising track.

If you decide to visit the windmill, short-cut to the lower road afterwards.

Pass a concrete block hut and keep climbing, reaching a notice about the SL FV 14 at the top of the track. A clear path continues up the stony slope, where the scrub is mainly sparse aulaga. The path winds as it climbs, and it is often stony or rocky but always obvious ahead. Views across the plains expand as height is gained, and tabaibal grows among aulaga further uphill. A final straight stretch rises to the broad gap of **Degollada del Marrubio**, at 583m (1913m). There is a trail shelter and picnic benches, and the GR 131 is also encountered, as described in Walk 41.

Walk down a track with aloes alongside, noting how bushes are crusted with lichens, drawing moisture from hillside mist. Walk

A last look back at Antigua before the path crosses the Degollada del Marrubio to reach Betancuria

The compact village centre of Betancuria boasts a fine range of interesting historic buildings

Betancuria is a popular village with accommodation, bar restaurants, museums, souvenir shops and buses.

down a road, Calle San Buenaventura, passing houses, then cut down to the right on a gravel path to Noria del Pozo de los Peña. Cross the road serving **Betancuria**, at 390m (1280ft), and go down a stone-paved road to spot a signpost on the left. Follow a narrow tarmac road and cross a riverbed. Go up a stone-paved path and steps, aiming for an old church in the historic centre of the village. Stone paving gives way to tarmac, reaching a signpost and mapboard. ◄

NORTH FUERTEVENTURA

Mountains rise above stony slopes near the village of Tefía (Walk 32)

The northern part of Fuerteventura is best accessed from the resort of Corralejo, or the island capital of Puerto del Rosario. Small mountain ranges appear much higher than they actually are, and the recent clearing and restoration of paths allows them to be explored relatively easily.

Interesting circular routes wander from village to village, crossing mountain passes and exploring valleys along the way. Walk 32 Links Casillas del Ángel and Tefía, while an extension can also include Tetir. Walk 33 links Tindaya, Vallebrón and La Matilla, while an extension can take in the remarkably rocky Montaña Tindaya. Walk 34 links the villages of Lajares and El Cotillo, then enjoys a there-and-back cliff coast walk to Playa de Esquinzo. Walk 35 makes a circuit from Lajares, following a popular path to the rugged crater of Calderón Hondo, and Walk 36 runs through the largely pathless sand dunes of the Parque Natural de Corralejo.

Three stages of the long-distance GR 131 run through this region, linking Valle de Santa Inés, Tefía, Tindaya, La Oliva, Lajares and Corralejo.

WALK 32
Casillas del Ángel, Tefía and Tetir

Start/Finish	Casillas del Ángel
Distance	14.5km (9 miles)
Total Ascent/Descent	550m (1805ft)
Time	4hrs 30min
Terrain	Mostly dirt roads and tracks. Mountain paths are mostly clear and easy, but occasionally steep and rugged.
Refreshment	Bar restaurants at Casillas del Ángel, and off-route at Tefía and Tetir
Transport	Regular daily buses serve Casillas del Ángel from Puerto del Rosario and Morro Jable. Occasional daily buses serve Tefía from Betancuria and Puerto del Rosario and serve Tetir from Puerto del Rosario, El Cotillo and Corralejo.

Despite climbing over three mountain passes, this is quite an easy walk. The passes are low and the paths crossing them are in good condition. The village of Casillas del Ángel is on the route, at the start and finish. Tefía is a little off-route, while Tetir is further off-route, visited by a short extension.

Route uses PR FV 15.

◀ Start at **Casillas del Ángel**, on a bend on the main road, near a large car park in front of two restaurants and a shop, around 210m (690ft). Face these buildings and find a signpost to the right, which points left for Tefía. Follow a quiet road left, watching for yellow/white flashes, avoiding turnings to left and right. Walk straight ahead along a dirt road at **Llano de las Pilas**, still avoiding turnings to left and right. Follow a track rising onto stony slopes dotted with sparse aulaga, enjoying views of the surrounding mountains. Reach a signpost on a crest, above **Degollada de la Vista de Casillas**, where there are views down to broad lowlands. Turn right up the track, and just after a cairn and a marker post around 300m (985ft), before the track climbs steeply, turn left.

A clear path quickly drops to a track, which slices across and gradually down bare, crumbling, gullied

slopes, which are later dotted with aulaga. Watch for a path marked to the left, which later rejoins the track. Turn left to continue down the track, passing a **waterworks** building and later reaching a signpost at a track junction. Turn right and follow a dirt road close to a farm; soon afterwards this becomes a tarmac road. A triangular road junction is reached at **Tefía de Arriba**, where there is a drystone-walled cactus garden. ▶ Turn right, now flashed red/yellow/white, and follow the road to the **Ermita de San Agustín**, where there are mapboards and signposts, around 200m (655ft). ▶

Turn right up a tarmac road that quickly becomes a track, swinging left and then right. Climb towards a goat farm on a hillside and keep right of it as marked. The track gives way to a path that climbs and swings left, twisting and turning on a bare, gullied slope. Eventually, it reaches a rocky little notch, crossing the gap of **Degollada de Facay** at 463m (1519ft). The path descends easily into a valley, crossing earth gullies on footbridges and reaching a viewpoint notice and a signpost. Follow a track past the little **Finca Mayola**, reaching another signpost at a track junction. Keep right to continue through the **Valle de Tetir**; the track is flanked by tumbled drystone walls and earth banks, and then by fences. Rise gently to a tarmac road and yet another signpost, at 310m (1020ft), at

Looking across the broad crest above the Degollada de la Vista de Casillas

The GR 131 is also signposted at this point. See Walk 42.

Tefía, with its bar restaurant and occasional buses, is 500m ahead.

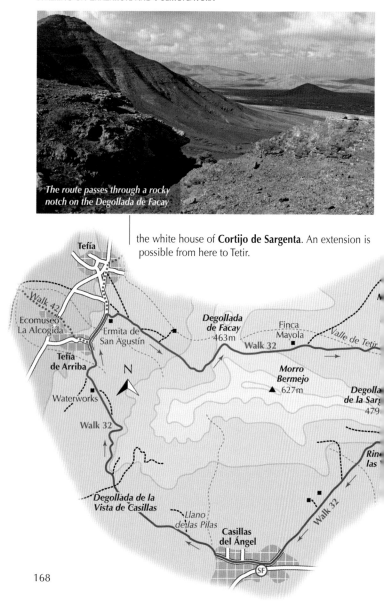

The route passes through a rocky
notch on the Degollada de Facay

the white house of **Cortijo de Sargenta**. An extension is
possible from here to Tetir.

Tefía

Walk 42

Ecomuseo
La Alcogida

Ermita de
San Agustín

Tefía
de Arriba

Waterworks

N

Walk 32

Degollada de la
Vista de Casillas

Llano
de las Pilas

Casillas
del Ángel

SF

*Degollada
de Facay*
463m

Finca
Mayola

Valle de Tetir

Walk 32

*Morro
Bermejo*
▲ 627m

Degolla
de la Sarg
479

*Rin
las

Walk 32

Extension to Tetir

This there-and-back excursion adds 5km (3 miles), and 100m (330ft) of ascent and descent, to the main route. Turn left up a dirt road signposted for Tetir. Cross a gap at 374m (1227ft) between Montaña de Tamateje and **Montaña de San Andrés**. Walk downhill with the village in sight, eventually reaching a tarmac road, buildings and a signpost. Turn right and follow the road into **Tetir**, reaching a church and plaza around 270m (885ft). A couple of bars are available, with a bus stop on the main road. Retrace steps to rejoin the main route in the Valle de Tetir.

Walk down from **Cortijo de Sargenta**, signposted for Casillas del Ángel. The track crosses the gentle valley floor and climbs, flanked by drystone walls, to reach a trail shelter, information board and signpost. A path climbs further with stone steps, eventually crossing the broad gap of **Degollada de la Sargenta** at 479m (1572ft) and turning sharp left. Splendid views take in villages and distant mountains. Walk down a narrow, rough, stony path on a steep, rocky, stony slope. There are 'tobacco' trees and verode on the slope. A track is crossed, but keep following the rugged path straight downhill. Eventually, join and follow a track more easily downhill, continuing straight along a dirt road flanked by low stone walls, with trees planted to the right. Pass a few houses and continue to the edge of **Casillas del Ángel**, where there is a signpost. Follow a road, bending right, and walk gradually down into the village to finish.

Tetir

Montaña de
San Andrés
▲
458m

563m
o de
alya

WALK 33
Tindaya, Vallebrón and La Matilla

Start/Finish	Tindaya
Distance	17km (10½ miles)
Total Ascent/Descent	530m (1740ft)
Time	5hrs
Terrain	Easy roads and tracks at the start and finish, but some rugged mountain paths in the middle.
Refreshment	Bar restaurants at Tindaya. Bar restaurant at La Matilla.
Transport	Occasional daily buses link Tindaya and La Matilla with Puerto del Rosario, La Oliva, El Cotillo and Corralejo.

The villages of Tindaya, Vallebrón and La Matilla are connected on this walk. A gentle mountain gap is crossed on the way to Vallebrón. Rugged slopes are crossed on the way to La Matilla, where the walk could be finished early. The route links with the GR 131 back to Tindaya, then Montaña Tindaya could be climbed as an 'extra'.

Route uses PR FV 9 and GR 131.

◀ Start in the village of **Tindaya**, where buses stop near the church, around 190m (625ft). A mapboard and signpost stand opposite. Follow the road out of the village, passing a junction where the Bar Cafeteria Maria is located. The road crosses a gently sloping area of stones and scrub, passing a white building to reach a junction with a main road. Turn left as signposted along a track running parallel to the road. Pass a tunnel where the road crosses the **Barranco de la Calabaza**. When a smaller tunnel is reached, go through it and then turn left to follow a path parallel to the road, later turning right along a track. Walk roughly parallel to a power line, then pass under it and follow a path further into a valley. Climb a couple of flights of log steps on a crumbling, stony slope to reach a viewpoint and noticeboard. Look back to Montaña Tindaya, then pass a mapboard and signpost on a broad, stony gap at 327m (1073ft).

Walk down a track into **Valle Chico**, passing culti-vated plots at first, then passing stony slopes that feature old terraces. A road-end is reached at some buildings and the road runs straight down through **Vallebrón**. Prickly pears and aloes grow beside many of the houses. Turn right at a road junction beside the Centro Cultural, and right again at the bottom beside a bus shelter, around 250m (820ft). Follow the road gently up through **Valle Grande**, flanked by palm trees. Eventually reach a junction where a signpost points left along a farm access road.

The road crosses a dip and then climbs and becomes a track, turning left and right before reaching a house on a hillside. Keep left and follow a path as marked, onto rugged, overgrazed slopes. Watch carefully for yellow/white markers while climbing, and take special care when a small bush is reached. The temptation is to follow a clear path straight ahead, but the route actually turns left, climbing and winding uphill, occasionally on crude stone steps. ▶ A longer flight of stone steps rises across the steep and rocky slope, then the path makes a sweep-ing zigzag across the **Degollada el Renegado**, at 502m (1647ft).

Stones and earth, washed down by rain, obscure the path in places.

Looking across Valle Grande on the climb to the Degollada el Renegado

The path runs gently down across a more vegetated slope bearing tabaibal, verode and aulaga. It traverses the steep slopes of a valley on **Montaña de la Muda**, then rises to cross a dirt road on a bare, stony shoulder, around 480m (1575ft). ◄ Follow a zigzag path downhill; it becomes more rugged as it runs beside aloes at **La Ladera**, reaching houses, a road and a signpost. Walk down the road and past one junction, then turn left at a crossroads. Walk to the main road at **La Matilla** and cross it, around 350m (1150ft). ◄ Continue along a quiet road flanked by palm trees, passing an ermita that could easily be missed.

The road gives way to a track, which reaches a fork where a left turn leads downhill. Follow this long track past the steep slopes of **Montaña de la Caldera** and **Rincón del Cercado**. Reach a junction with a dirt road where the GR 131 is joined. ◄ Turn right and follow the dirt road gently down and then gently uphill. It is briefly covered in tarmac past an isolated **house**, and reaches a signpost. Turn left down a path flanked by stony scrub, pass a little farm with a windpump and follow a track past a signpost to reach a road. Turn right and then quickly left to cross the road, then walk up another track as signposted. Gradually climb the bright, stony slope of **Tablero Blanco**, which bears very little scrub. Keep left at a junction and follow the track towards a gap at the foot of **Montaña Quemada**. ◄ A curious dwelling lies to the right of the track, around 220m (720ft). The track crosses a slight dip and then reaches a road at the top end of **Tindaya**.

Walk towards the village, but turn left along Calle de la Casa Alta as signposted. The road swings right and passes a cheese-making business. Walk straight ahead and downhill through three crossroads, almost as if bypassing the village. However, continue to a crossroads where there is a shop, bar and signpost. Either finish here, or climb nearby Montaña Tindaya.

Extension to Montaña Tindaya
This optional route is 3km (2 miles) in length and involves 220m (720ft) of ascent and descent. Walk

This serves a military installation high on the mountain.

A bar restaurant lies to the right.

This could be followed left to Tefía.

Another track climbing left leads to a statue of the Spanish poet, novelist and playwright Don Miguel de Unamuno – who was exiled to Fuerteventura in 1924 for criticising the new government of General de Rivera.

straight towards the mountain; the road soon bends left and goes through a crossroads, later reaching a fork. Keep right along a tarmac road, then fork right along a dirt road. Turn left to reach a parking space at the foot of the mountain, where a signpost reads 'Sendero

The steep and rocky slopes of Montaña Tindaya can be climbed after the main circuit

Subida Montaña Tindaya'. Follow a path up to some ruined buildings, keeping left to pass behind them, to climb a narrow path on steep and stony slopes. There is sparse scrub and occasional clumps of prickly pears, with bare rock at a higher level, where the path drifts left of the ridge and zigzags vaguely on steep slopes of stones and rock. Later, follow a rocky ridge further uphill, keeping right to pass below the 399m (1309ft) summit, therefore making a sharp left turn to reach it. The top of **Montaña Tindaya** is well vegetated, mainly with verode, and views extend around Fuerteventura into Lanzarote. Carefully retrace steps.

WALK 34

Lajares, El Cotillo and Playa de Esquinzo

Start	Lajares
Finish	El Cotillo
Distance	9.5 or 22km (6 or 13½ miles)
Total Ascent	100m (330ft)
Total Descent	150m (490ft)
Time	3 or 7hrs
Terrain	Sandy tracks and dirt roads, then a gentle cliff path and an option to finish on tracks.
Refreshment	Plenty of choice in Lajares and El Cotillo.
Transport	Regular daily buses link Corralejo, Lajares and El Cotillo. Occasional buses also link with Puerto del Rosario.

This easy walk links the villages of Lajares and El Cotillo, passing through a deserted and desert-like landscape. An early finish is possible at El Cotillo, where the second half of the route features a fine, easy cliff-top walk to the remote beach of Playa de Esquinzo, returning to El Cotillo.

▶ Start at the roundabout and bus stops on the western side of **Lajares**. ▶ Walk away from the village towards the main road, for three options. One is to turn right and walk along the road; another is to turn right and walk parallel to

Route uses PR FV 1.

There are shops, bar restaurants, an ATM and buses here.

the road on sandy ground. A third option follows a sandy track

map continues on page 177

175

away from the roundabout, short-cutting a corner. Assuming that the road is followed, pass the **Km31** marker and walk until a mapboard and signpost are seen on the left.

Walk onto the broad, sandy bed of the **Barranco de la Cañada de Melián**. The bed usually features wheel-marks, and the gentle slopes alongside are covered with low, bushy scrub. Yellow/white marker posts are occasionally seen to right and left, but simply follow the broad bed straight ahead. Two tracks cross from side to side; don't follow either of them, but stay in the bed of the barranco, noting that the second track passes two huts built of concrete blocks. Eventually the broad bed splits into three and a signpost points right along the gritty, stony bed of the **Barranco de Cho Cruz**. ◀ Later, another signpost points right up a stone-paved ramp, where a notice explains about the birdlife. There is a view of La Oliva, but this is lost to sight as a track is followed uphill, crossing stone-paved fords. The slopes are stony, riven by small gullies and sparsely dotted with scrub such as aulaga.

A fenced area alongside is used for studying birds.

The bed of the gentle Barranco de la Cañada de la Melián, and Montaña de la Mareta

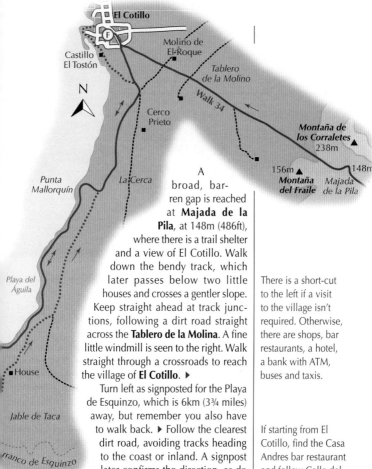

A broad, barren gap is reached at **Majada de la Pila**, at 148m (486ft), where there is a trail shelter and a view of El Cotillo. Walk down the bendy track, which later passes below two little houses and crosses a gentler slope. Keep straight ahead at track junctions, following a dirt road straight across the **Tablero de la Molina**. A fine little windmill is seen to the right. Walk straight through a crossroads to reach the village of **El Cotillo**. ▶

Turn left as signposted for the Playa de Esquinzo, which is 6km (3¾ miles) away, but remember you also have to walk back. ▶ Follow the clearest dirt road, avoiding tracks heading to the coast or inland. A signpost later confirms the direction, as do occasional yellow/white markers.

Later, another signpost points right along a stony track, soon giving way to a path flanked by parallel lines of stones. A fine view stretches along beaches to El Cotillo, as well as inland to low, rounded hills. The path has a rope fence alongside at **Punta Mallorquín**, where the cliff is collapsing.

There is a short-cut to the left if a visit to the village isn't required. Otherwise, there are shops, bar restaurants, a hotel, a bank with ATM, buses and taxis.

If starting from El Cotillo, find the Casa Andres bar restaurant and follow Calle del Castillo.

A gentle path runs along cliff-tops from El Cotillo to Playa de Esquinzo

If you go down the steps, beware the danger of rockfall.

The path is easy to follow, staying a safe distance from the edge and barely rising and falling. Look down to a sandy beach at **Playa del Águila**, then pass a signpost and walk above concrete steps bearing a safety notice. ◀ The path runs through hummocky rubble and then turns round **Punta de Taca**, enjoying fine views. Pass a line of fenceposts without wire between them, and note a house a short way inland. Continue along the cliffs to reach a mapboard above the sandy **Playa de Esquinzo**. Either retrace steps to El Cotillo, or move inland a little to follow tracks that link with the dirt road back to the village. Feel free to visit the cliff-edge tower of **Castillo El Tostón** and the headland round the edge of the village.

WALK 35

Lajares and Calderón Hondo

Start/Finish	Football ground, Lajares
Distance	10km (6¼ miles)
Total Ascent/Descent	200m (655ft)
Time	3hrs 15min
Terrain	Mostly along easy roads, tracks and stone-paved paths, with only one short, steep climb.
Refreshment	Plenty of choice at Lajares.
Transport	Regular daily buses link Lajares with Corralejo and El Cotillo. Occasional buses also link with Puerto del Rosario.

Old volcanoes rise above Lajares, and a popular path heads for Calderón Hondo. A viewpoint allows walkers to look down into a deep crater from a breach in its rim. A stretch of the GR 131 can be followed back to Lajares, though it is also possible to follow it in the other direction to Corralejo.

▶ Start at a roundabout where there is also a football ground and bus stop, on the eastern side of **Lajares**,

Route uses SL FV 2 and GR 131.

A clear track rises across the slopes of Montaña Colorada

There are shops, bar restaurants, cafés, ATM and buses in the village.

around 75m (245ft). ◀ A signpost points up Calle Majanicho, the road beside the football ground, which goes to the last houses in the village. There is a small car park here, beside a mapboard and signposts. Walk along a track with a stone-paved strip along its centre. Bend to the right as marked by green/white flashed marker posts, rising across the reddish slopes of **Montaña Colorada**.

Continue past a turning area, around 150m (490ft), later reaching the end of the track. A stone-paved path continues across a rugged, stone-strewn area, reaching a junction. Turn left along another stone-paved path, signposted for **Calderón Hondo**, and keep turning left at junctions to climb a steep, rocky slope to a breach in the crater rim of the volcano. There is a telescope here, at 230m (755ft) for studying the view.

Go back downhill, and consider taking the second stone-paved path to the left, just to look at a curious stone-built **hut**. Otherwise, return to the signpost for Calderón Hondo, then turn left and follow a stone-paved path, passing a mapboard. Reach a dirt road and a signpost, around 180m (590ft) on a broad gap, facing into the crater of **Caldera de Rebanada**. ◀ Turn right to follow the dirt road downhill, passing a white building and later turning right as marked at one junction, then right again as signposted at another junction, around 115m (380ft). Rise a little and pass a trail shelter and picnic tables, then continue along the bendy, undulating track called Calle Juanita.

Turning left leads to the bustling resort of Corralejo. See Walk 44.

A little **house** lies to the right of the track, where there is a surprising amount of vegetation, and then an information board is passed, detailing the view towards the mountains from **Cuesta de la Caldera**. Later, two modern houses are passed – one on the left and one on the right – then a tarmac road is joined and followed past a few more houses. Turn right at a signposted road junction, along Calle Montaña Colorada. Turn right again at a way-marked road junction, along Calle El Fragosito. ▶ This becomes a dirt road, and a left turn leads back to the little car park, mapboards and signpost on Calle Majanicho. Turn left down the road into **Lajares**.

It is possible to short-cut straight to Calle Majanicho.

WALK 36
Parque Natural de Corralejo

Start	El Porís
Finish	El Campanario, Corralejo
Distance	8km (5 miles)
Total Ascent/Descent	50m (165ft)
Time	2hrs 30min
Terrain	Mostly bare sand dunes, but covered in scrub near Corralejo.
Refreshment	Plenty of choice at Corralejo.
Transport	Regular daily buses link Corralejo and the Riu Oliva Hotel, but they don't stop at El Porís, so use a taxi.

The Parque Natural de Corralejo is a miniature sandy desert within easy reach of the bustling resort of Corralejo. Buses pass it, but only stop at the Riu Oliva Hotel. However, a quick taxi ride reaches the start of this walk at El Porís. From there, make a beeline back to Corralejo, enjoying rolling sand dunes and arid scrub.

Start at **El Porís**, where there is a roadside car park between the Km19 and Km20 markers. All the beaches near Corralejo get busy, but the extensive Dunas de

Pathless, wind-blown sand dunes rise inland from El Porís, with Montaña Roja rising to the south

Corralejo attract only a few wanderers – some of them naked! Walk inland onto the highest nearby dune, just to see if Corralejo can be spotted. Two whirling wind turbines might be noticed, and it is a simple matter to walk towards them, checking and amending the direction whenever the crest of another dune is crossed. There may be footprints all over the place, but no real path.

The area is called **El Jable** (The Sand) and it is unlikely that the route climbs as high as 30m (100ft). By all means walk barefoot, but there are sharp shell fragments in the sand. Small ranges of mountains lie to the south and west, while the Riu Oliva complex is the only development clearly in view, with the hump of Lobos beyond and Lanzarote in the distance. The sand is mostly bare, but there are occasional bushes and straggly 'tobacco' trees. Eventually, the route draws level with the Riu Oliva complex, passing a **power line**. Aim for a little more height in order to see ahead to Corralejo. Note the two wind turbines, but also look for the prominent tower of El Campanario. ◄

If you have already visited the Campanario Shopping Centre, you will recognise its tower easily..

Although there is still plenty of sand, it becomes increasingly covered in thorny scrub. There is no need to

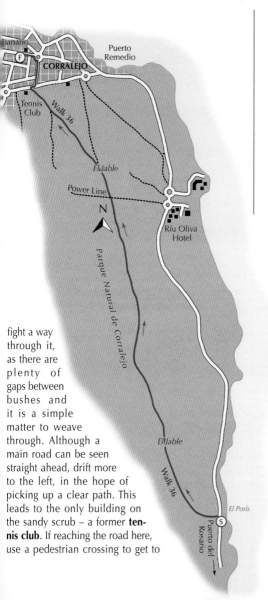

fight a way
through it,
as there are
plenty of
gaps between
bushes and
it is a simple
matter to weave
through. Although a
main road can be seen
straight ahead, drift more
to the left, in the hope of
picking up a clear path. This
leads to the only building on
the sandy scrub – a former **tennis club**. If reaching the road here,
use a pedestrian crossing to get to

Bare sand is traversed at first, but scrub increases on the way towards Corralejo

the other side. Turn right and then left to follow Calle Lanzarote to a roundabout, where there are bus stops to the right. If continuing into **Corralejo**, the nearest big feature – the **El Campanario** Shopping Centre – is to the left.

GR 131 – EL PUERTITO TO ISLA DE LOBOS

A trail shelter on the GR 131 in the Barranco de Bácher near the village of Cardón (Walk 40)

The long-distance GR 131 traverses all seven of the Canary Islands, and the stretch through Fuerteventura is the longest at 154km (95½ miles). It also includes a short hop from Corralejo to the tiny Isla de Lobos. The route is quite varied, covering some remote and arid areas, such as the Jandía peninsula and desert-like Istmo de la Pared, as well as the busy resorts of Morro Jable and Corralejo. In-between, stages link small villages and explore mountain ranges and low-lying plains that separate them.

The provision of simple trail shelters at intervals offers relief from strong sun and wind, while most villages offer at least a small bar for refreshment. The villages of Pájara, Betancuria and La Oliva offer plenty of historical interest. Accommodation isn't available at every stage along the GR 131, and while it is possible to 'commute' to most parts of the trail by bus, there are a few places where this is difficult, so drop-offs and pick-ups would need to be organised.

The GR 131 links with most of the day walks on Fuerteventura, so it is possible to see what the route is like before following it.

WALK 37

GR 131 – Punta de Jandía to Morro Jable

Start	Punta de Jandía
Finish	Promenade, Morro Jable
Distance	20km (12½ miles)
Total Ascent/Descent	250m (820ft)
Time	5hrs
Terrain	Low-level coast and hillsides. Arid, barren, stony, sandy and occasionally rocky slopes.
Refreshment	Café at Punta de Jandía. Bar restaurants at El Puertito. Plenty of choice at Morro Jable.
Transport	Ask for a 4WD taxi at Morro Jable as normal taxis won't travel on the dirt road. Regular daily buses serve Morro Jable from Puerto del Rosario. Ferry services link Morro Jable with Gran Canaria.

Punta de Jandía is a remote and barren rocky point, with the tiny village of El Puertito only serving to highlight its remoteness. The route is mostly coastal for the first half of this stage, then it rises to traverse the lower slopes of a mountain range, finishing in the busy little port resort of Morro Jable.

Start on the **Punta de Jandía**, where the lighthouse, Faro Punta de

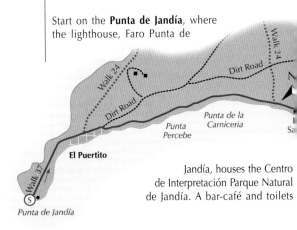

Jandía, houses the Centro de Interpretación Parque Natural de Jandía. A bar-café and toilets

stand alongside. A mapboard and signpost mark the beginning of the GR 131. Look round the battered cliffs, with stony desert stretching inland to a serrated range of mountains. ▸ Follow a broken tarmac road, or the low cliffs, to the ramshackle village of **El Puertito**. The village was founded by fishermen and offers a couple of bar restaurants specialising in fish dishes. Reach a junction of battered tarmac roads with signposts. ▸

Keep straight ahead, following the GR 131 along the road to a prominent wind turbine. Turn right and follow a track to the coast, swinging left while walking away from the village. Cross low cliffs such as **Punta Percebe** and **Punta de la Carniceria**. There are small beaches of grey shingle or golden sand. Marker posts help distinguish the route where two or three paths and tracks run parallel, and abundant 'X' markers indicate which ones shouldn't be followed. The correct path is usually closest to the sea. The ground undulates gently, but there is a short, steep, stony descent to a broad track near a car park at **Las Salinas**. ▸

The coastal path is signposted onwards, passing a few little houses and huts at **Cueva de Negra**. Follow the rugged, undulating path, passing a couple more stone huts. The path becomes more convoluted as it crosses rugged little barrancos, where there are also short, steep, stony descents and ascents. Two broad vehicle tracks drop to two large sandy beaches, and the second one, **Playa de Juan Gómez**, features a dirt car park on a headland. Continue as

These are explored on Walks 24, 25 and 26.

Walk 24 heads left for Las Talahijas.

Camping is allowed, but there are no facilities.

map continues on page 188

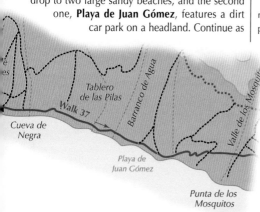

Little sandy beaches are passed on the way to the large sandy beach of Playa de Juan Gómez

marked and pass a signpost. When passing another small beach, the path runs close to the circular stone base of a ruined limekiln.

Head inland, where the path winds and climbs and then rises more gently towards the mountains. The walking is mostly easy and the path is flanked by parallel lines of stones. Markers show the continuation every time a track is

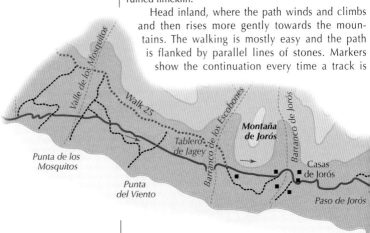

crossed. There is a bendy stretch, then after crossing the little **Valle de los Mosquitos**, look up to the left to spot clumps of spiky cardón de Jandía. Keep walking onwards, mostly gently uphill, until the path swings left and drops into the broad, stony **Barranco de los Escobones**. Climb from this towards a ruined concrete building beside the dirt road serving the peninsula.

The route rises gradually inland and later crosses the Valle de los Mosquitos

Turn right to follow the road, only as far as you can see, to a nearby bend. Turn left as signposted up and along a rugged path that later drops to the road beside a white building. There are a few other buildings, former cultivated plots, a couple of palm trees, tamarisks and spurge-like trees at the **Casas de Jorós**. Turn left to follow the road

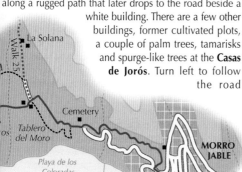

round a bend, passing a mapboard. Follow the road away from the buildings and across stony slopes where there are only little tufts of scrub. Watch for a GR 131 signpost on the right, where a clear path leaves the road at **Paso de Jóros**.

The path gradually drifts away from the road, crossing tracks and dry streambeds. A group of buildings are approached, but before reaching them the path swings left and returns to the dirt road. ◄ Cross over and climb straight uphill as marked. When a path junction is reached, turn right, and the route appears to head straight towards the ferryport at Morro Jable. However, the path suddenly bends in all directions to cross two barrancos and then climbs to a **cemetery** where there are a number of palm trees.

Spot a signpost just beyond the cemetery, then follow a path that rises gradually from the road. Drop into a barranco near a road bend and climb steeply from it. The path reaches a small orange tower marking the course of a buried pipeline. Turn right to follow the path past more orange structures, running almost level across a steep and rugged slope above the **ferryport**. The path bends round gullies of black basalt, contrasting with spurs of golden calcareous sandstone. When the path runs near a waterworks, a steep and stony descent leads to a signpost and main road.

Cross over the road, turn right, and watch for a red-and-white flashed path veering away from the road past a few palm trees. The path quickly reaches a tarmac turning space; walk up the road and through a crossroads, where there are interesting palms, cacti, cardón and dragon trees. The road ahead is signposted 'Centro Urbano', and red/white flashes appear on lamp posts. Turn right at a junction, then left down Calle Altavista. Turn right along Calle los Guanches and go down steps beside a modern white church. A paved path and more steps lead into narrow passageways in the resort of **Morro Jable**. ◄ Walk to a promenade path above the beach, passing bars and restaurants. A mapboard and signpost are reached where a floodwater channel runs beneath the promenade.

A left turn leads to the start of Walk 25.

There is a full range of services and facilities in and around the resort.

WALK 38

*GR 131 – Morro Jable to
Barranco de Pecenescal*

Start	Promenade, Morro Jable
Finish	FV-2 road, Barranco de Pecenescal
Distance	16km (10 miles)
Total Ascent	400m (1310ft) plus 40m
Total Descent	350m (1150ft)
Time	5hrs
Terrain	Built-up resorts separated by rugged barrancos, then arid, stony, sandy ground.
Refreshment	Plenty of bars and restaurants at first, then fewer later.
Transport	Regular daily buses serve Morro Jable and nearby resorts, as well as Barranco de Pecenescal, from Puerto del Rosario.

This stage comes in two distinct halves. The morning is spent walking from one resort to another, taking in numerous hotels, apartments, 'clubs', restaurants, bars and cafés; the second half is wilder, with ever-increasing amounts of wind-blown sand, so that it looks like uninhabited desert towards the end.

Start on the brick-paved promenade in **Morro Jable** and follow it over a rise. Palm trees lie to the left, offering shade, while a steep sandbank lies to the right, towering above the beach. Alternatively, walk along the sandy beach. The promenade later levels out and runs beside the beach; either turn left to continue along the promenade, or continue along the sandy **Playa del Matorral**. ▸

Note that there are three paths allowing walkers to switch between both options. After the first two, the beach can flood at high tide.

> An enormous saltmarsh, the **Saladar de Jandía**, sits between the promenade and beach. This is a site of scientific interest with no public access.

The promenade is divided into pedestrian and cycle lanes, running parallel to the busy FV-2 road. The main

The GR 131 follows a footpath/cycleway below the Iberostar complex at Jandía Playa

path linking the promenade and beach is at the lighthouse, **Faro** de Morro Jable, where there is a beach bar.

The promenade later passes a small grassy space where the skeleton of a sperm whale, 16m (52½ft) long, is mounted. The **Zoo Park** lies inland among masses of palm trees. More notices about the saltmarsh are passed as the promenade runs past the resort of **El Matorral**. When the Ventura Shopping Centre is seen, an underpass on the left is signposted for Pico de la Zarza, climbed on Walk 26. Stay on the promenade, which reaches the end of the saltmarsh and continues beside the beach at **Jandía Playa**. Note how the sprawling Iberostar complex follows the shape of the slope and attempts to match the colour of the sand.

Tides permitting, it is possible to continue along the beach, which is both sandy and rocky.

The promenade ends and the route briefly steps onto the beach. ◄ Soon head inland, however, up a dirt road through the **Valluelo de la Cal**. This isn't at all scenic, having been completely bulldozed. The main FV-2 road is joined at the top and followed to bus shelters and a roundabout, where lots of statues of children have been planted, around 40m (130ft). There are two ways to proceed, depending on the state of the tide, which will have been noticed at the last beach.

High tide option
If the tide is fully in, pass the roundabout and follow a dirt road running parallel on the right.

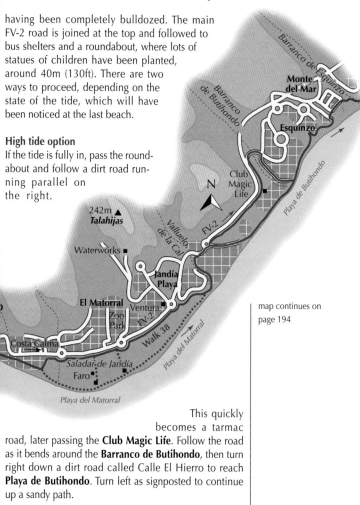

map continues on
page 194

This quickly becomes a tarmac road, later passing the **Club Magic Life**. Follow the road as it bends around the **Barranco de Butihondo**, then turn right down a dirt road called Calle El Hierro to reach **Playa de Butihondo**. Turn left as signposted to continue up a sandy path.

Low tide option
If the tide is out, leave the roundabout and walk down Calle Melindraga, continuing down a track to reach a

193

beach bar. Walk along the sandy beach, where red/white flashes have been painted onto rocks. Circular windbreaks are passed, made from beach cobbles. Space to walk here would be limited at high water, and some of the cliffs are undercut, making escape difficult. The broad mouth of the **Barranco de Butihondo** is crossed to reach a beach bar at **Playa de Butihondo**. Turn left inland, as signposted up a sandy path.

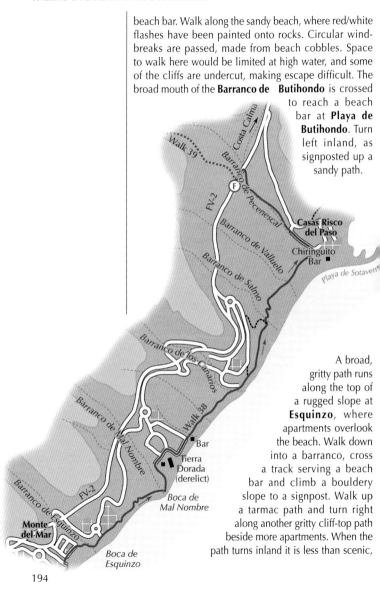

A broad, gritty path runs along the top of a rugged slope at **Esquinzo**, where apartments overlook the beach. Walk down into a barranco, cross a track serving a beach bar and climb a bouldery slope to a signpost. Walk up a tarmac path and turn right along another gritty cliff-top path beside more apartments. When the path turns inland it is less than scenic, but turn right and follow a road, Calle Volcán de Vayuyo, straight down through **Monte del Mar**. Turn right when almost at the bottom to follow a path parallel to the white boundary wall of a restaurant. The path drops steeply to a sandy beach. Turn left to pass a building and a beach bar.

Either walk along the beach, which is easy when the tide is out, or look carefully to spot red-and-white flashed marker posts revealing a little-trodden path across a steep sandbank. If the beach is followed, pass the foot of a flight of steps. If the marked path is followed, walk down the steps and turn left along the beach. Pass wind-break shelters built from beach cobbles and turn left into a rocky little barranco. Zigzag up a path as marked on a steep and stony slope. Keep left of a derelict building and pass a signpost. Walk along and down a path on a stony slope bearing very little scrub. After all the built-up resorts, the GR 131 returns to the wilds.

Zigzag down into and up from a barranco where there is beach access. Cross an elevated area, then drop into the broader **Barranco de Mal Nombre**, where there is a fine sandy beach. Climb to a signpost and turn left inland, soon joining a road. Follow this over a rise in an area containing a derelict development and quarried, bulldozed land, around 40m (130ft). Turn right down another road, then left down a dirt road to reach a beach bar at **Tierra Dorada**. Walk along the beach – little more than a wave-washed slope of cobbles backed by a steep sandbank.

A little valley is reached and a path climbs from the beach. After a slight drop into another little valley the path climbs to around 40m (130ft). Walk down again, into the broad, scrub-filled **Barranco de los Canarios**. ▶ A large unfinished development overlooks the barranco. Climb a broad, brick-paved path, avoid the development, and watch for red/white flashes along a path. This is a little rugged later, but then it runs more gently above 40m (130ft), with desert-like views ahead featuring bare sandbanks and hills covered in wind-blown sand. A narrow sandspit encloses the shallow Laguna de Sotavento, explored on Walk 27. Walk down to a track

There is a beach car park and toilets, but no bar.

and cross it, then swing left as marked, up into a barranco, crossing it too.

A path climbs steeply, covered in windblown sand. Enjoy views ahead again, then go down to the **Barranco del Salmo**, which is full of sand. Cross it and climb another steep, sandy path, with more desert-like views ahead. Look down on saltmarshes and ahead to the lagoon and a huddle of white houses. Walk down to a big sandy car park before the **Casas Risco del Paso**, where there is a mapboard and a signpost. Turn right if the Chiringuito Bar is required, with its sand floor and woven cane walls, otherwise turn left inland. ◄ Walk along the sandy bed of the **Barranco de Pecenescal**, which is surprisingly firm. The sand is calcareous and after getting wet it can set like concrete. When the bed forks, turn right and go through a tunnel beneath the main **FV-2 road**. Turn left to follow a fence over a crest above the road, then come down to a road junction around 50m (165ft).

Walk 27 continues along the beach.

The trail crosses increasingly desert-like terrain on the way towards the Casas Risco del Paso

There is no nearby accommodation, but plenty of buses run along the road to towns, villages and resorts with lodgings. There are bus stops in lay-bys on both sides of the road. Buses go fast along this road, so give a very clear signal to stop one.

WALK 39
Barranco de Pecenescal to La Pared

Start	FV-2 road, Barranco de Pecenescal
Finish	La Pared
Distance	16km (10 miles)
Total Ascent/Descent	270m (885ft)
Time	5hrs
Terrain	Gently graded dirt roads and sandy tracks, but rough and stony in places.
Refreshment	A few bar restaurants around La Pared.
Transport	Regular daily buses serve the Barranco de Pecenescal from Puerto del Rosario and southern resorts. La Pared has a limited bus service of little use to walkers. Use a taxi to link with buses at Costa Calma.

The GR 131 spends a whole day traversing the narrow, hilly Istmo de La Pared. There is sandstone underfoot and wind-blown sand everywhere. The scrub is very sparse, leaving the landscape looking like a desert. A taxi pick-up at La Pared is likely to be needed at the end of the day.

Start on the busy FV-2 road at bus lay-bys near the **Barranco de Pecenescal**. Follow a dirt road signposted for Pecenescal, reinforced with a GR 131 signpost, passing between two large noticeboards. ▶ Sand lies everywhere, and the only vegetation to thrive are succulent *tetraena* bushes. Cross a gentle rise where a pylon line crosses, then descend gently into the broad, stony Barranco del Valluelo, where 'tobacco' trees bind the gravel in the streambed.

Small notices advise that the land alongside is important for birds.

197

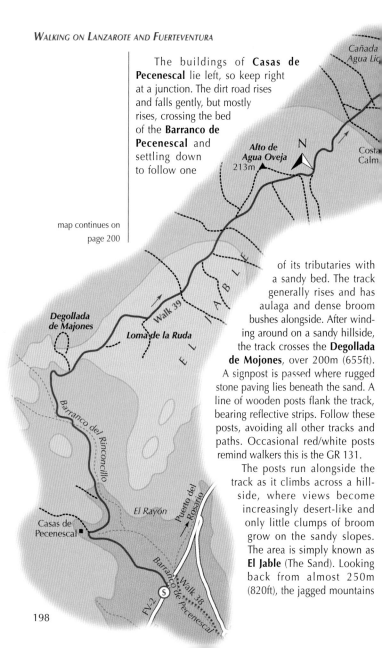

Cañada
Agua Lic

The buildings of **Casas de Pecenescal** lie left, so keep right at a junction. The dirt road rises and falls gently, but mostly rises, crossing the bed of the **Barranco de Pecenescal** and settling down to follow one

Alto de Agua Oveja 213m

N

Costa
Calm

map continues on page 200

Degollada de Majones

Loma de la Ruda

Walk 39

E L   J A B L E

Barranco del Rinconcillo

Casas de
Pecenescal

El Rayón

Puerto del Rosario

Barranco de Pecenescal

Walk 38

FV-2

S

of its tributaries with a sandy bed. The track generally rises and has aulaga and dense broom bushes alongside. After winding around on a sandy hillside, the track crosses the **Degollada de Mojones**, over 200m (655ft). A signpost is passed where rugged stone paving lies beneath the sand. A line of wooden posts flank the track, bearing reflective strips. Follow these posts, avoiding all other tracks and paths. Occasional red/white posts remind walkers this is the GR 131.

The posts run alongside the track as it climbs across a hillside, where views become increasingly desert-like and only little clumps of broom grow on the sandy slopes. The area is simply known as **El Jable** (The Sand). Looking back from almost 250m (820ft), the jagged mountains

of the Jandía peninsula look very attractive. There is a long and gradual descent, with more mountains seen far ahead and wind turbines to the right. It becomes increasingly sandy on the descent, then there is a gentle ascent across the slopes of **Alto de Agua Oveja**, at almost 200m (655ft).

The track levels out and descends a little, then rises as if heading for a gentle hill. However, the track swings left and descends again, passing sparse clumps of aulaga and broom. A low part of the isthmus is reached, around 80m (260ft), where a signposted dirt road crosses. ▶ The GR 131 continues straight ahead, over a slight rise, now with fewer wooden posts alongside (now flashed red/white). The track is also rough and stony in places. The lowest part of the crest is reached around 60m (200ft). The track runs straight ahead, climbing gently past tetraena bushes and cutting across the upper slopes of **Granillo**. There is a sudden right and left turn onto a broad dirt road at **Piedras Negras**, around 100m (330ft). The surface is now grit and gravel.

Follow the dirt road over a gentle crest, then cross another dirt road and continue straight along a sandy

Halfway across El Jable, Costa Calma could be reached from a signposted intersection of tracks

A right turn leads to the resort of Costa Calma and the main road and bus services in less than an hour.

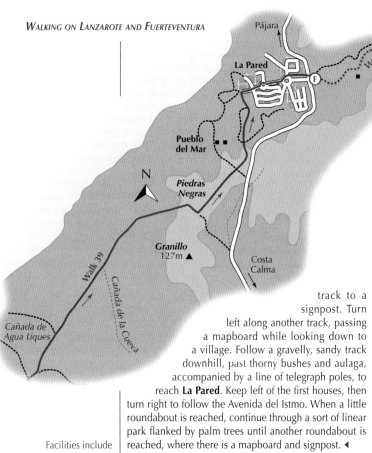

track to a
signpost. Turn
left along another track, passing
a mapboard while looking down to
a village. Follow a gravelly, sandy track
downhill, past thorny bushes and aulaga,
accompanied by a line of telegraph poles, to
reach **La Pared**. Keep left of the first houses, then
turn right to follow the Avenida del Istmo. When a little
roundabout is reached, continue through a sort of linear
park flanked by palm trees until another roundabout is
reached, where there is a mapboard and signpost. ◄

Turn left down the road, but quickly turn right up
the stony bed of a barranco. Pass tamarisk bushes, then
go through the middle eye of a bridge and walk straight
ahead along a track as marked, where there is also a sign
for 'Queso Artesano'. This is easily seen from the road at
the top end of La Pared.

Facilities include
a shop and bar
restaurants, but no
accommodation.
Buses aren't much
use, so call for a taxi
if moving off-route.

WALK 40

GR 131 – La Pared to Pájara

Start	La Pared
Finish	Church, Pájara
Distance	24km (15 miles)
Total Ascent	850m (2790ft)
Total Descent	700m (2295ft)
Time	8hrs
Terrain	Easy tracks at first, then stony paths, tracks and roads. Later, rugged mountain paths with many ascents and descents. Easy tracks and roads at the end.
Refreshment	Bar and café at Cardón. Plenty of choice at Pájara.
Transport	Limited bus services to La Pared, Cardón and Pájara. Check timetables carefully or arrange drop-off and pick-up.

This stage starts easily, but becomes a little more rugged later. The village of Cardón has little to offer walkers; beyond it, the route climbs into rugged little mountains, where it follows an arid, exposed, uninhabited crest. Pájara can often be seen in the distance, and tracks later allow the village to be reached more quickly.

Start at the top end of **La Pared**, at a junction with the main road, where a dirt road bears a sign reading 'Valle de La Pared'. Walk only a few paces along the dirt road, then turn right where a big sign reads 'Queso Artesano'. The dirt road rises gently and the ground alongside is grey, stony, gravelly and gritty, bearing crinkly aulaga. Pass a couple of dwellings

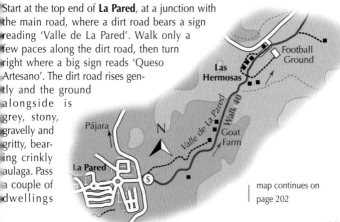

map continues on page 202

A track leads through the Barranco de las
Hermosas, passing occasional farms and houses

Goats and sheep are milked nearby, and as there is no grazing left, fodder and water have to be provided.

and a cheese factory. ◄ The dirt road rises to a football ground at **Las Hermosas**, and just across a tarmac road lies the chapel of San Benito de Abad, where a few trees offer shade.

Don't step onto the tarmac road, but stay on the dirt road, rising further. Keep straight ahead at a junction and cross a crest. Walk down the other side, rise again, and keep straight ahead at junctions through the **Barranco de las Hermosas**. Avoid tracks leading to properties and briefly follow a short stretch of tarmac road, continu-

There are fine views of Montaña de Cardón ahead.

ing gently up a track running parallel to a road. ◄ Just before reaching the road, head for a solitary white gateway marked 'Huertas de Chilegua'. Walk up a stony streambed and turn left as marked to reach the road near a tumbled ruin. Turn right to continue parallel to the road,

Walking on the road is easier.

though it does mean walking on stones and crossing crumbling gullies. ◄

Pass a house with a fine cactus garden, and later join a tarmac access road and follow it up through a cutting. Turn right down another road, go round a left-hand bend and later turn left up a track as marked. Join a clearer track to climb back to the road at a signpost. Turn right to walk parallel to the road, though it is very stony. The highest part of the road is over 280m (920ft), at **Cantil del Esquén**, and a final house is passed. A track is marked running down from the road, later bending left and right, passing an enclosure. Watch for a path on the left, climbing a steep slope bearing aulaga and returning to the road. ▸ Go through a gap in the roadside barrier to cross the road, then turn right and walk behind the barrier on the other side to reach a signpost.

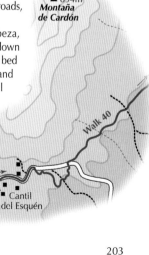

Stay on the road to avoid the descent and re-ascent.

A path leaves the road, descending gently across stony slopes with fine views of distant hills. Undulate, crossing a dry streambed and passing sparse scrub – except where hollow areas have been dammed, where greenery flourishes. The path is washed-out in dry streambeds, so watch for its continuation. Look up the steep and rocky slopes of **Montaña de Cardón** to see swathes of cardón growing. Eventually, reach a trail shelter with picnic benches, beside a circular corral.

A signpost points ahead past a barrier. Walk down a steep track and continue along a road, then turn left along another track and climb a steep road. Red and white markers are found on lamp posts. Level out on the Camino de Julian Castillo Francés and turn right to walk down into **Cardón**. There is a bus shelter at a crossroads, but very few buses.

map continues on page 204

Walk straight along the Camino de Vista Cabeza, past a bar and church, signposted for Pájara. Step down to the right later to continue along a dirt road in the bed of a barranco. Tarmac roads climb right and left, and a mapboard on the left highlights the SL FV 53 trail (see Walk 28 for details). The dirt road passes the last few buildings in the

▲ 694m
Montaña de Cardón

Walk 40

Barranco de las Hermosas

Rincón de las Hermosas

Cantil del Esquén

Football Ground

N

Barranco de Bácher, then a trail shelter and signpost lie to the right.

The path swings right and climbs a steep, stony slope to a marker post on the crest of **Filo de Cuchillo Negro**, over 310m (1015ft). Enjoy views across plains to distant hills, taking in villages, houses and farms. Turn left and follow the path beside or along the crest as it bends and undulates, then climb stone steps past tabaibal. The route doesn't quite reach the summit of **Morro de Moralito**, at 414m (1358ft). A couple of benches and a signpost are passed, then the path runs easily beside a fence, dropping on a steep, bouldery slope. Stay near the fence, crossing a rugged slope below a rounded summit

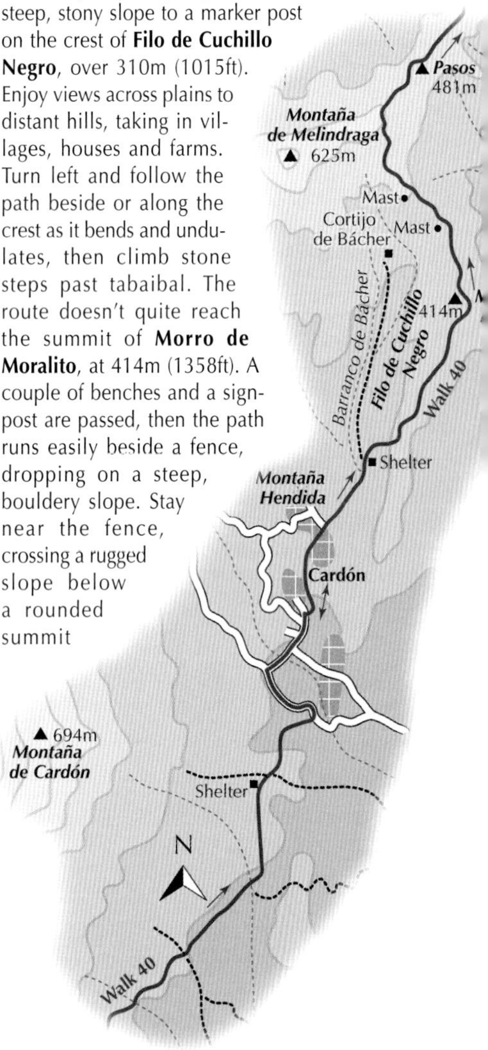

▲ **Pasos** 481m

Montaña de Melindraga
▲ 625m

Mast •
Cortijo Mast •
de Bácher ■

▲ 414m

Barranco de Bácher

Filo de Cuchillo Negro

Walk 40

■ Shelter

Montaña Hendida

Cardón

▲ 694m
Montaña de Cardón

Shelter ■

N

Walk 40

map continues on page 206

204

Looking across the settled lowlands from the high crest of Filo de Cuchillo Negro

crowned with a tall **mast**. Later, leave the fence as marked and climb towards another **mast**, but avoid a track leading to it, instead using a waymarked path avoiding it.

Rejoin the fence and follow it to a corner, then follow a low stone wall uphill. Go through a gap in the wall and catch a glimpse of distant Pájara and Toto. The path climbs past rugged old terraces, then rejoins the low stone wall and crosses it around 500m (1640ft) on Cuchillo de los Pasos. Walk down a steep, crumbling slope to a gap. The ridge ahead is very rocky, but the path slips to one side, passing huge boulders below rocky buttresses. ▶ Pass a trig point at 481m (1578ft) on the summit of **Pasos** and enjoy views of arid hills all around.

Follow a broad, rocky, stony ridge gently downhill. The path is vague in places, but clear enough to be spotted ahead. It runs down to a gentle gap and then makes a short, steep climb. Cross a rounded crest bearing two vague tops on **Filo de Tejeda**, then drop to the gap of **Degollada Honda**. A short, steep climb leads to a cairn shelter, followed by a slight dip, and then there is a longer climb on a rounded, stony crest to 450m (1475ft). Ahead is **Montaña de la Fuente**, but don't climb it; turn left instead as marked. A narrow path drops towards the **Barranco Hondo**, where there is a solitary palm tree. Cross a little valley where there is a rubble dam, then a short, steep,

The rocks hold sufficient moisture to allow a range of plants to flourish, not seen on nearby arid slopes.

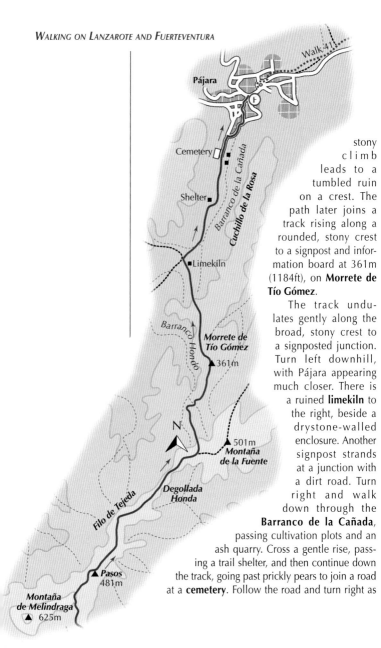

stony climb leads to a tumbled ruin on a crest. The path later joins a track rising along a rounded, stony crest to a signpost and information board at 361m (1184ft), on **Morrete de Tío Gómez**.

The track undulates gently along the broad, stony crest to a signposted junction. Turn left downhill, with Pájara appearing much closer. There is a ruined **limekiln** to the right, beside a drystone-walled enclosure. Another signpost strands at a junction with a dirt road. Turn right and walk down through the **Barranco de la Cañada**, passing cultivation plots and an ash quarry. Cross a gentle rise, passing a trail shelter, and then continue down the track, going past prickly pears to join a road at a **cemetery**. Follow the road and turn right as signposted at a junction, following Calle los Geranios into **Pájara**. Pass the Museo de Tahona, based on a simple mill. Turn right at the end of the road and follow Calle la Cañada into the village centre. A plaza with shady trees is followed by another plaza, with more trees, beside a church. ▶

There is accommodation, a bank with ATM, shops, bar restaurants, buses and taxis here.

WALK 41

GR 131 – Pájara to Betancuria

Start	Church, Pájara
Finish	Bus stop, Betancuria
Distance	17km (10½ miles)
Total Ascent	710m (2330ft)
Total Descent	520m (1705ft)
Time	5hrs 30min
Terrain	Easy valley walking, then a rugged mountain gap. More easy valley walking, then a climb into the mountains.
Refreshment	Bar restaurants at Vega de Río Palmas and Betancuria.
Transport	Daily buses link Vega de Río Palmas and Betancuria with Tefía and Puerto del Rosario.

After an easy walk from Pájara to Toto, the route continues into a rugged valley and crosses a mountain gap. An easy walk through Vega de Río Palmas is followed by the recreational area of Castillo de Lara. After climbing into the mountains the route descends to the ancient village of Betancuria.

Leave the church in **Pájara** and follow Calle Nuestra Señora de Regla, as if heading for Betancuria. Cross a bridge over a riverbed, pass a roundabout and follow the road for Toto, which is flanked by palm trees. When a pedestrian crossing is reached, step down to the left into a dry riverbed. Turn right as signposted and follow the bed of the **Barranco de Toto** past cultivated plots. Later, turn left up a road into the village of **Toto**, climbing the steep Calle Cuesta de San Antonio. Pass a little church and shady plaza, keep straight ahead uphill, then descend a little to the end of the tarmac. A track continues to a signpost, where a path continues into the **Barranco de Teguereyde**.

The restored path crosses bare rock for a while, then passes a goat-grazed enclosure where stout tabaibal grow. The path undulates while running parallel to a track serving

Vega de Río Palmas

Río Palmas

Walk 29 *Barranco de las Peñitas*

La Banda

Ermita *Presa de las Peñitas*

Valle de los Granadillos

Walk 41

Degollada los Granadillos 479m

■ Shelter

Barranco de Teguereyde

Walk 41

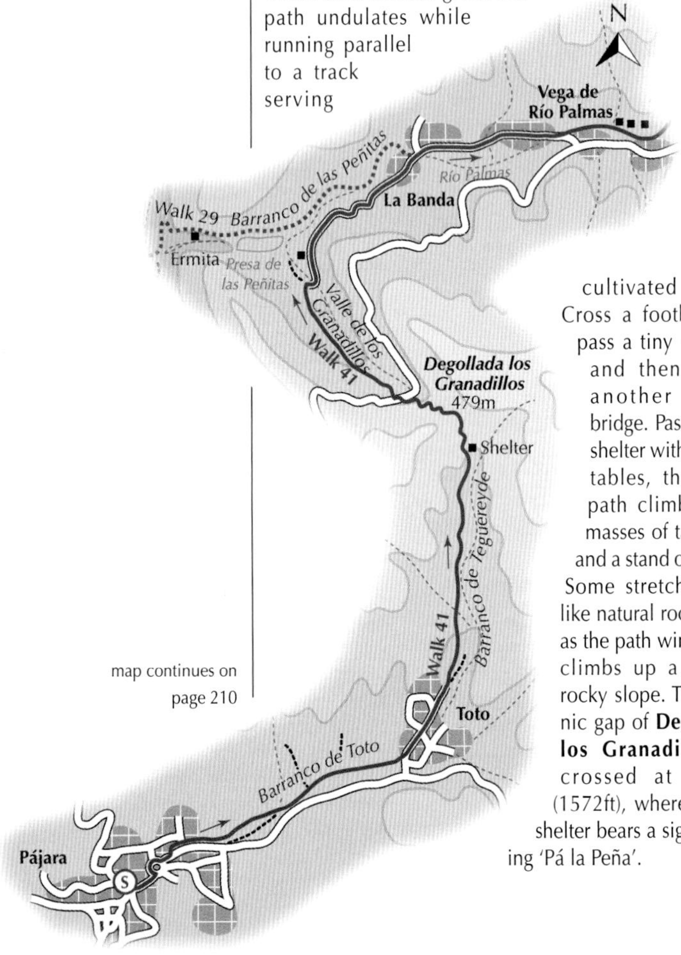

map continues on page 210

Toto

Barranco de Toto

Pájara

cultivated plots. Cross a footbridge, pass a tiny shelter and then cross another footbridge. Pass a trail shelter with picnic tables, then the path climbs past masses of tabaibal and a stand of aloes. Some stretches are like natural rock steps as the path winds and climbs up a steep rocky slope. The scenic gap of **Degollada los Granadillos** is crossed at 479m (1572ft), where a tiny shelter bears a sign reading 'Pá la Peña'.

Descend a stony slope bearing sparse aulaga and asphodels, with a view of a winding mountain road. Cross the road as signposted to follow a steep, rugged path winding down a rocky, bouldery slope covered in mixed scrub in the **Valle de los Granadillos**. Reach a few fruit trees, a building and lots of palm trees. Continue down a rugged track to a junction, then turn right along a quiet minor road. Enjoy views of the **Barranco de las Peñitas**, reaching houses and a bus stop at **La Banda**. Cross a bridge to reach a car park and signposts. ▶

Walk 29 leads through the barranco to Ajuy.

Follow the road up through the long and straggly village of **Vega de Río Palmas**, passing the Tapa Bar and a bus shelter. Continue past a play park, signpost and shop. Leave the houses to cross a bridge, then turn left as signposted along the broad, dry bed of **Río Palmas**. Walk until there are signposts on both sides, where there is access to bar restaurants and the church of the Virgen de la Peña.

> The **church** was built as an easier option for pilgrims, instead of visiting an ermita deep in the rocky Barranco de las Peñitas.

If not visiting the village, keep following the dry riverbed as signposted for Betancuria. The next signpost is for Agua de Bueyes and Tiscamanita, where it is possible to climb and join Walk 30. However, stay in the riverbed, passing another signpost and walking straight ahead. The bed is broad and gravelly, flanked by tamarisk and palm

Scrub bushes and pines are encountered on the way to the recreational area of Castillo de Lara

trees. When it becomes rocky on the right, turn right as marked, following a narrow, gravel streambed past canes, palms, tamarisk and boulders. Go through a **tunnel** beneath a road and turn right up stone steps to a noticeboard and signpost. Turn left up a dirt road, rising gently at first then steepening as it swings into the **Barranco del Acebuche**, where trees and bushes grow.

There is a view of an **Aula de la Naturaleza** centre ahead, but the route turns left beforehand at a signpost. Climb a steep and rugged path on a stony, rocky slope of mixed scrub. Pass left of a hillside building and go behind it. Walk along an easy path across a gentle dip, following an overhead line to a pylon. Continue straight ahead and gently down across a bushy slope, later passing lots of blasted pine trees. Go down steps into a forested valley to the recreational area of **Castillo de Lara**. ◄ Pass above it and climb steps to a signpost. Turn right up a forest track and climb to the top of it.

Go through a gate in a fence and notice how a line of aloes

> This features barbeque areas, picnic benches, water, toilets and a play park.

runs parallel to the fence. The gap of **Degollada de los Pasos** stands at 568m (1864ft), with a view down the other side to Antigua. Turn left to follow the track up a rounded, stony crest bearing sparse scrub. The track goes through the fence, but don't follow it, instead continuing up a path. The track later comes back through the fence and is followed across a rounded top. Continue across a dip, then climb to the top of **Morro del Cortijo**, at 637m (2090ft), where there is a cairn shelter. ▶

Views include the villages of Antigua and Betancuria, with all the surrounding hills.

The fence heads down to the left, so follow a path along the rounded crest, passing windbreak shelters and descending to the gap of **Degollada del Marrubio**, at

Aloes flank the track descending from Degollada del Marrubio to Betancuria

583m (1913m). There is a trail shelter and picnic benches, and Walk 31 also crosses here, between Antigua and Betancuria. Turn left and walk down a track with aloes alongside, noting how bushes are crusted with lichens, drawing moisture from hillside mist. Walk down a road (Calle San Buenaventura), passing houses, then cut down to the right on a gravel path to Noria del Pozo de los Peña. Cross the road serving **Betancuria**, at 390m (1280ft), and go down a stone-paved road to spot a signpost on the left. Follow a narrow tarmac road and cross a riverbed. Go up a stone-paved path and steps, aiming for an old church in the historic centre of the village. Stone paving gives way to tarmac, reaching a signpost and mapboard. ◀

This is a popular village with accommodation, bar restaurants, museums, souvenir shops and buses.

WALK 42
GR 131 – Betancuria to Tefía

Start	Bus stop, Betancuria
Finish	La Cancela, Tefía
Distance	18km (11 miles)
Total Ascent	340m (1115ft)
Total Descent	530m (1740ft)
Time	6hrs
Terrain	An ascent and descent, then mostly low-level, following roads, dirt roads and tracks, with occasional stony paths.
Refreshment	Bar restaurants at Valle de Santa Inés. Café at La Alcogida. Restaurant at Tefía.
Transport	Daily buses serve Betancuria, Valle de Santa Inés, Llanos de la Concepción and Tefía from Puerto del Rosario.

The route climbs from Betancuria, crosses a mountain pass, and then runs down towards lowlands. Easy dirt roads and tracks lead from village to village, passing Valle de Santa Inés and Llanos de la Concepción to reach Tefía. The Ecomuseo La Alcogida can be explored towards the end of the day.

Start at the bus stop below the church in **Betancuria**, around 390m (1280ft). A mapboard and signpost stand

beside a small car park, and the GR 131 is signposted for Corralejo. Cross the road, which is also a bridge, and follow a narrow road beside a streambed. Turn right, then quickly left up the road, later passing above the ruined **Ermitas** de San Diego y San Francisco and a water-works building. Continue up the road, then fork left as signposted along a track. This is flanked by aloes as it climbs, followed by tabaibal, aulaga and occasional acacia trees. Almost join a road at a junction (which climbs to the Mirador de Morro Velosa and its summit café), but follow a path to the left, crossing a road on top of a gap at **Corral de Guize**, at 588m (1929ft).

Behind the statues a signpost indicates a rugged path running roughly parallel to the road, down across a rugged, scrubby slope. The path soon descends more directly than the road, following a rounded crest and

Statues of Guise and Ayose, Fuerteventura's last Guanche chieftains, stand at Corral de Guize

map continues on page 214

213

straggly fence. The path winds and is trodden to bedrock later. Continue along a track through a cultivated valley, crossing it and rising to a signpost. Keep right to walk down a tarmac road. Keep right again at a road junction, walking down across the valley side and later crossing it again. Reach another road junction and signpost, turning right to follow a bendy road that also rises and falls, over and over. Another right turn leads to a roundabout, shop, a couple of bar restaurants and bus stop at **Valle de Santa Inés**, around 280m (920ft).

Turn left, but don't follow the road out of the village. Follow a dirt road running

Valle de las Cuevas

Walk 42

Llano de Leme

Llanos de la Concepción

Lomo del Cabrito

Windmill

Lomo de Tetir

map continues on page 216

Valle de Santa Inés

La Cuesta del Valle

N

Corral de Guize

588m

parallel, later veering away from the road. Avoid turnings to left and right, and keep walking straight ahead as marked. Note a **windmill** to the left while descending to a dirt crossroads and signpost.

Keep straight ahead, then turn left along a rubble riverbed to pass beneath old and new road. (The main road heading left reaches a shop/bar and bus stop.) Turn left up a short track onto a road and walk past a church at **Llanos de la Concepción**, around 200m (655ft). Turn right at a crossroads and pass a fine cactus

garden at La Era Vieja, then continue straight along a dirt road. Pass exhausted stone-walled plots and continue along a road heading gently down and uphill.

Reach a crossroads and follow a dirt road straight ahead. This passes lots of widely spaced lookalike houses, then there is a final white house as the dirt road bottoms out, around 140m (460ft). The broad **Barranco de los Molinos** looks like a scrubby semi-desert, but during wet spells, water flows into a nearby reservoir – Embalse de los Molinos. Follow the dirt road gently uphill and keep right of a property surrounded by acacia trees. Pass a small building and turn right at a junction, then continue until another junction is reached. Turn left and continue rising gently, with the reddish slopes of **Montaña Bermeja** to the right. The dirt road later becomes a private access road, so turn right as signposted, following a track up a light-coloured stony slope and traversing round the foot of the mountain. A trail shelter is reached beside a drystone enclosure.

Continue rising gently along the stony track, across a scrubby semi-desert, then head gently down to cross a road. Follow a path on the other side, turning right as

View across a barren, stony plain near Montaña Bermeja, with distant Tefía in view

215

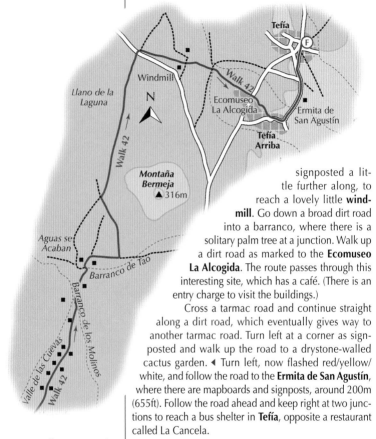

Tefía

Windmill

Llano de la
Laguna

N

Walk 42

Walk 42

Ecomuseo
La Alcogida

Ermita de
San Agustín

Tefía
Arriba

Montaña
Bermeja
▲ 316m

Aguas se
Acaban

Barranco de Tao

Barranco de los Molinos

Valle de las Cuevas

Walk 42

Walk 32 joins at this
point.

signposted a lit-
tle further along, to
reach a lovely little **windmill**. Go down a broad dirt road
into a barranco, where there is a
solitary palm tree at a junction. Walk up
a dirt road as marked to the **Ecomuseo
La Alcogida**. The route passes through this
interesting site, which has a café. (There is an
entry charge to visit the buildings.)

Cross a tarmac road and continue straight
along a dirt road, which eventually gives way to
another tarmac road. Turn left at a corner as signposted and walk up the road to a drystone-walled
cactus garden. ◀ Turn left, now flashed red/yellow/
white, and follow the road to the **Ermita de San Agustín**,
where there are mapboards and signposts, around 200m
(655ft). Follow the road ahead and keep right at two junctions to reach a bus shelter in **Tefía**, opposite a restaurant
called La Cancela.

WALK 43

GR 131 – Tefía to La Oliva

Start	La Cancela, Tefía
Finish	Church, La Oliva
Distance	18km (11 miles)
Total Ascent	250m (820ft)
Total Descent	230m (755ft)
Time	5hrs 30min
Terrain	Mostly along low-level dirt roads and tracks, with short linking paths.
Refreshment	Restaurant at Tefía. Bar restaurants at Tindaya and La Oliva.
Transport	Daily buses serve Tefía from Betancuria and Puerto del Rosario. Daily buses serve Tindaya from El Cotillo, La Oliva and Puerto del Rosario. Regular daily buses serve La Oliva from El Cotillo and Corralejo, with fewer from Puerto del Rosario.

The whole of this day's walk is low-level and easy, mostly following dirt roads. The only village passed during the day is Tindaya, at the foot of Montaña Tindaya. An ascent of this remarkable little mountain is recommended. The village of La Oliva is where the military rulers of Fuerteventura once lived, at Casa de los Coroneles.

Start from the bus stop at La Cancela in **Tefía**, around 200m (655ft). Follow the road only to the edge of the village, quickly reaching a signpost for the GR 131. Turn right down a dirt road, which undulates, avoiding turnings to adjacent properties. Note that the route is flashed red/yellow/white on marker posts. Cultivated plots are passed, but the stony slopes of **El Rincón de Hija** are dotted with scrub. Turn left down past the Happy Plants garden centre to reach a

El Piquito
545m ▲

Cañada de Martínez

N

Lomillo Cumplido

El Rincón de Hija

Tefía

Walk 43

map continues on page 219

junction and signpost. Turn right and follow a dirt road past an enclosure of young trees, crossing a rise and overlooking a goat farm. The dirt road rises again to reach a signposted junction at the foot of **El Piquito**, over 200m (655ft). ◀

Walk 33 joins at this point and turning right leads up to La Matilla.

Keep left, or straight ahead, to follow the dirt road gently down and gently uphill. It is briefly covered in tarmac past an isolated **house**, reaching a signpost. Turn left down a path flanked by stony scrub, pass a little farm with a windpump, and follow a track past a signpost to reach a road. Turn right and quickly left to cross the road, then walk up another track as signposted. Gradually climb the bright, stony slope of **Tablero Blanco**, which bears very little scrub. Keep left at a junction and follow the track towards a gap at the foot of **Montaña Quemada**. ◀ A curious dwelling lies to the right of the track, around 220m (720ft). The track crosses a slight dip and then reaches a road at the top end of **Tindaya**.

Another track climbing left leads to a statue of Don Miguel de Unamuno – exiled to Fuerteventura in 1924.

Walk towards the village, but turn left along Calle de la Casa Alta as signposted. The road swings right and passes a cheese-making business. Walk straight ahead

The village of Tindaya and the rocky little mountain of Montaña Tindaya

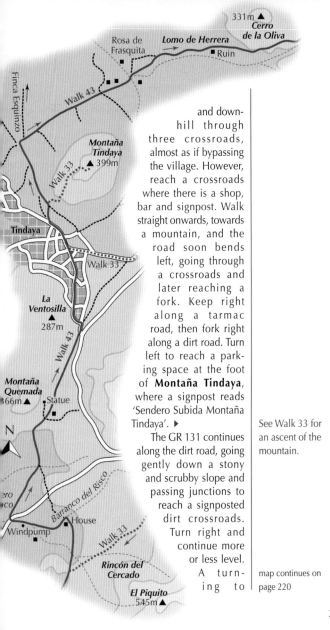

and downhill through three crossroads, almost as if bypassing the village. However, reach a crossroads where there is a shop, bar and signpost. Walk straight onwards, towards a mountain, and the road soon bends left, going through a crossroads and later reaching a fork. Keep right along a tarmac road, then fork right along a dirt road. Turn left to reach a parking space at the foot of **Montaña Tindaya**, where a signpost reads 'Sendero Subida Montaña Tindaya'. ▶

See Walk 33 for an ascent of the mountain.

The GR 131 continues along the dirt road, going gently down a stony and scrubby slope and passing junctions to reach a signposted dirt crossroads. Turn right and continue more or less level. A turning to

map continues on page 220

the left is marked for Finca Esquinzo, so keep straight ahead. A very gentle rise and descent leads to an area with a few farm buildings and another signposted dirt crossroads at **Rosa de Frasquita**. Keep straight ahead, pass a goat farm and cross a dip around 140m (460ft). Climb gradually up a bright, stony, semi-desert slope with sparse scrub. ◄ Continue rising, with an occasional slight descent, and note a ruin to the right, with a village ahead. The scrub alongside is bushier as the track levels out, flanked by drystone walls.

A notice near a tumbled ruin details the view of mountains ahead.

Reach a tarmac road and turn left alongside buildings. Turn right at a signposted crossroads; the road being followed bends right, with houses on both sides. Reach a junction at **Villa de los Artistos**, where a grove of palm trees shades scantily clad statues. Turn left to reach a

LA OLIVA

The Casa de los Coroneles at La Oliva was once occupied by the military rulers of Fuerteventura

Military rule on Fuerteventura was once administered from the Casa de los Coroneles, now a museum. There is also an arts centre and a thriving market. Facilities include accommodation, post office, bar restaurants, pizzeria, regular buses to Corralejo and El Cotillo and occasional buses to Puerto del Rosario.

crossroads and a main road, where a filling station has a café. Cross the main road and walk straight along another road, free of buildings until it reaches a junction. Turn right to walk into the sprawling village of **La Oliva**, aiming for a crossroads, plaza and a prominent church, around 220m (720ft).

WALK 44
GR 131 – La Oliva to Corralejo

Start	Church, La Oliva
Finish	Harbour, Corralejo
Distance	25km (15½ miles)
Total Ascent	255m (835ft)
Total Descent	455m (1490ft)
Time	8hrs
Terrain	Roads and dirt roads, with a few steep and rugged paths.
Refreshment	Bar restaurants at La Oliva and Lajares. Plenty of choice at Corralejo
Transport	Regular daily buses serve La Oliva and Lajares from El Cotillo and Corralejo. Occasional buses also serve those places from Puerto del Rosario.

The route traverses two 'malpais' regions, which feature rugged old lava flows. Between La Oliva and Lajares, the Monumento Natural Malpais de la Arena is passed. Between Lajares and Corralejo, the Malpais de Bayuyo is crossed. The GR 131 makes its way through the suburbs and centre of Corralejo to reach the harbour.

Leave **La Oliva** by following the main road for Corralejo. Pass the Museo Aloe Vera and reach a signposted road junction. Turn left, walk straight along a road, turn right as marked and then left as signposted. Check directions throughout by watching for red/white flashes on lamp posts. The road rises gently and a track continues beyond the last buildings. The way is later barred to

The GR 131 rises gradually to pass beside Montaña de Arena, above La Oliva

map continues on page 223

vehicles and has been converted into a walled path, rising past walled, scrub-filled fields, to a bend on a dirt road near **Montaña del Molino**. Only a few paces along the dirt road, turn left as signposted along another walled path, rising past rugged old lava flows and later crossing a track where a notice announces the Monumento Natural **Malpais de la Arena**. The path rises to a dirt road and two signposts.

Turn left up the dirt road, passing old fields surrounded by drystone walls. Some contain aloes and prickly pears, while tiny enclosures contain fig trees. Cross a rise and reach a fork, heading left uphill, around 280m (920ft), then down to a trail shelter. ▶ Turn left at the shelter and almost immediately right at a 'malpais' notice, down a narrow path. Although the path winds, it is quite direct and broadens to become a track passing small grassy fields. Turn right as signposted along a track, then quickly turn left and walk down a dusty, white dirt road. There is a building to the left, then later the horse-riding centre of **Finca Julie** lies to the right. Next on the right is the **Finca Ecologica**, then a pronounced bend on the track can be short-cut.

Views extend to Corralejo, Lobos and Lanzarote.

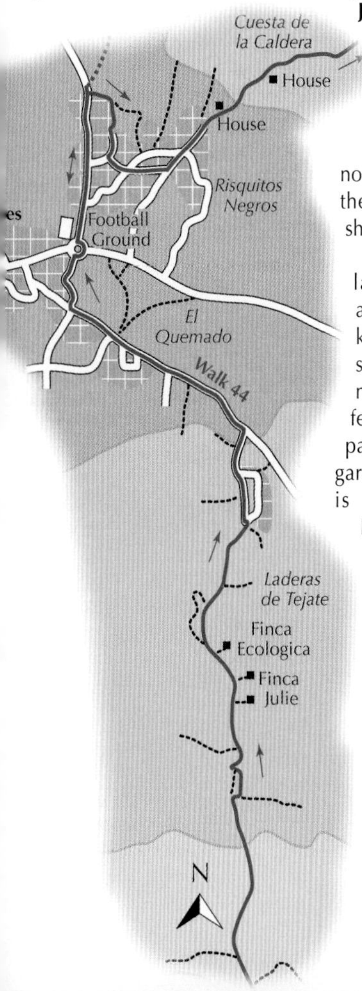

The dirt road later becomes a tarmac road, keeping left of several houses, many of which feature spacious palm and cactus gardens. The road is Calle Gavias Nuevas, and it drops to a signposted junction. Turn left to follow the road towards more houses. At first there are just a few houses to the left of the road; when there

Map labels:
Cuesta de la Caldera
House
House
Risquitos Negros
es
Football Ground
El Quemado
Walk 44
Laderas de Tejate
Finca Ecologica
Finca Julie
N

map continues on page 224

223

The village has shops,
bar restaurants, ATM
and buses.

Walk 35 could be
followed, rejoining
the GR 131 after
visiting Calderón
Hondo.

are houses on both sides, turn right along Calle los
Quemados, reaching a roundabout on the edge of the
sprawling village of **Lajares**, around 75m (245ft). ◀

A signpost points up Calle Majanicho, the road
beside the football ground, up to the last houses in the
village. There is a small car park here, beside a mapboard
and signposts. ◀ Turn right for the GR 131, following a
track called Calle los Cascajos. Turn right at Calle El
Fragosito and follow this as marked. The dirt road
becomes tarmac and reaches a road junction.
Turn left, then fork right at another junction
as marked, along Calle Montaña Colorada.
Follow the road down to a junction and
signpost, then turn left and follow the
road until it passes another signpost and becomes a dirt road
called Calle Juanita.

Two modern
houses are
passed – one
on the left
and one

on the
right – then
a stony track
continues past
broken old lava
flows. Later, an
information board
is passed, detailing
the view towards the
mountains from **Cuesta de
la Caldera**. A small house
lies to the left, where there is

a surprising amount of vegetation. The track passes a trail shelter and picnic tables, then drops a little to join a dirt road at a signpost. Turn left and follow the dirt road to a junction, then turn left again and follow it up past a white building to a broad gap, around 180m (590ft), beside the crater of **Caldera de Rebanada**. ▶

Follow the dirt road gently downhill, overlooking little farms, with views to Lanzarote. ▶ Stay on the dirt road, which bottoms out around 100m (330ft) and then climbs to overlook a green hollow. A notice points out some of the features in view, such as a nearby cave and hills. Pass more green hollows among the stony slopes, then the dirt road climbs over a gap, around 130m (425ft), and runs down past a crater on the flanks of **Bayuyo**. A sign on the right reads 'Caldera', and it is easy to walk off-route a few paces to look inside. The dirt road rises gently and then descends, passing a stockade-like structure. Next, a notice explains about farming methods on **Morro Francisco**. After passing a building, the route reaches the road network of a failed urban development.

Turn right along a road equipped with pavements and lamp posts, but few buildings. Walk up to a road junction, turning left to walk down to a roundabout bearing a sail-like sculpture, with a signpost and mapboard alongside. Turn left and walk beside a busy road, straight towards **Corralejo**. The Avenida Juan Carlos I eventually has buildings on both sides. Keep walking, preferably on the left-hand side of the road, until a sign reading 'Muebles Ojeda' projects from a furniture store. ▶ Turn right to use a pedestrian crossing and follow the narrow Calle Lepanto, where the GR 131 is occasionally flashed red/white on lamp posts. There is a glimpse of the sea

Walk 35 joins here, and could be followed in reverse to visit the crater of Calderón Hondo.

One of the farms, Las Calderas, offers goats' cheese.

This is just before the bus station.

A green hollow is passed at Morros Tamboriles, and then there is a gradual descent to Corralejo

ahead, but turn left beforehand, along the narrow Calle La Milagrosa. This leads to a plaza, mapboard and sign-post. Head for the **harbour** beyond to check ferry timetables for the Isla de Lobos.

WALK 45
GR 131 – Isla de Lobos

Start/Finish	El Muelle, Isla de Lobos
Distance	11km (6½ miles)
Total Ascent/Descent	250m (820ft)
Time	3hrs
Terrain	Clear tracks and paths, mostly easy, but steep and rugged on the mountain.
Refreshment	Restaurant at El Puertito.
Transport	Regular daily ferries serve Isla de Lobos from Corralejo. There are nearly always ferries from Corralejo at 1000, and from Lobos at 1600. If planning to stay longer, check whether there are later ferries.

The GR 131 includes a 3.5km (2¼ mile) walk across the Isla de Lobos, but walkers have to return to the ferry. Retracing steps is one option, but it is better to return a different way. In fact, the island is worth a thorough exploration, and short paths allow salinas and beaches to be visited, and a small mountain to be climbed.

The ferry between Corralejo and Lobos takes about 15 minutes. Step onto a pier at **El Muelle** and have a look at a mapboard detailing paths around the island, which is designated as the Parque Natural Islote de Lobos. There is a fork, where the GR 131 heads left, but if the **visitor centre** ahead is open, have a look inside first. Follow the track and keep left at a junction, and later keep right. When an information board is reached at a fork, it is worth heading left to visit the former **Salinas de Marrajo**.

Retrace steps and continue along the main track, crossing a gentle rise to reach yet another signposted junction. Again, turning left is well worthwhile, following a path across a level area, then climbing a steep and stony path and steps on **Montaña de la Caldera**. Enjoy views from

The dry and empty evaporation pools at the Salinas de Marrajo

227

Views embrace Lobos, northern Fuerteventura and southern Lanzarote.

Note how the hilltop was adapted so that rainwater could collect in a cistern.

the trig point at only 123m (404ft), then retrace steps to the main track. ◄

Continue walking, rising and falling between tiny hills and hollows, to reach a junction at the final GR 131 mapboard and signpost. Walk up to a lighthouse, **Faro de Lobos**, and look across the sea to Lanzarote, where the GR 131 continues. ◄ Walk back to the mapboard and junction, then use the other path, signposted for Las Lagunitas and El Puertito. This is slightly more stony and sandy, and it passes a couple of ruins. Keep right at a junction, following the clearest path, and later note a dense stand of aloes to the left. Later, cross a stone-built water channel. The track eventually descends in a hairpin bend to the tidal saltmarsh of **Las Lagunetas**.

After a while the track forks: the right-hand option is the shortest, while the left-hand option is better for exploring the rugged coast. Both rejoin to continue past shabby little buildings at **El Puertito**, where there is a little restaurant specialising in fish. Follow arrows to the left to find the restaurant, otherwise keep straight ahead to return to the pier at **El Muelle**, following clear signposts.

Looking towards the Isla de Lobos and Montaña de la Caldera from Corralejo

APPENDIX A

Route summary table

No	Start	Finish	Distance	Time	Total Ascent	Total Descent	Page
Lanzarote							
1	Roundabout, Femés	Roundabout, Femés	8km (5 miles)	2hrs30	430m (1410ft)	430m (1410ft)	33
2	Roundabout, Femés	Roundabout, Femés	10km (6¼ miles)	3hrs	410m (1380ft)	410m (1380ft)	36
3	Roundabout, Femés	Roundabout, Puerto Calero	12km (7½ miles)	3hrs30	270m (885ft)	610m (2000ft)	39
4	Roundabout, Femés	Avenida Marítima, Playa Blanca	23km (14¼ miles)	7hrs	230m (755ft)	600m (1970ft)	43
5	Avenida Marítima, Playa Blanca	El Golfo	25km (15½ miles)	8hrs	150m (490ft)	150m (490ft)	48
6	Aljibe, Yaiza, or Juan Perdomo	Teatro Tinajo, or Playa de la Madera	30 or 13km (18½ or 8 miles)	10 or 5hrs	300 or 50m (985 or 165ft)	300 or 50m (985 or 165ft)	53
7	Correos, Mozaga	Church, Uga	21.5km (13½ miles)	7hrs	370m (1215ft)	430m (1410ft)	59
8	La Florida	La Florida	9km (5½ miles)	3hrs	100m (330ft)	100m (330ft)	64
9	Mancha Blanca	Mancha Blanca	21 or 24km (13 or 15 miles)	6 or 7hrs	230 or 480m (755 or 1575ft)	230 or 480m (755 or 1575ft)	68
10	Plaza de San Roque, Tinajo	Caleta de Famara	15km (9½ miles)	4hrs30	20m (65ft)	240m (790ft)	73

No	Start	Finish	Distance	Time	Total Ascent	Total Descent	Page
11	Church, Tiagua	Caleta de Famara	16km (10 miles)	5hrs	20m (65ft)	220m (720ft)	78
12	Windmill, Teguise	Caleta de Famara	11km (6¾ miles)	3hrs	20m (65ft)	320m (1050ft)	81
13	Los Zocos Club Resort, Costa Teguise	Los Zocos Club Resort, Costa Teguise	7km (4½ miles)	2hrs	230m (755ft)	230m (755ft)	84
14	Windmill, Teguise	Bar El Bulín, Guatiza	18km (11 miles)	5hrs30	220m (720ft)	430m (1410ft)	86
15	Arrieta	Caleta de Famara	18.5km (11½ miles)	6hrs	650m (2130ft)	650m (2130ft)	91
16	Las Rositas, near Ye	Las Rositas, near Ye	8km (5 miles)	3hrs	380m (1245ft)	380m (1245ft)	96
17	Caleta del Sebo	Caleta del Sebo	16km (10 miles)	5hrs	410m (1345ft)	410m (1345ft)	100
18	Caleta del Sebo	Caleta del Sebo	19km (12 miles)	6hrs	250m (820ft)	250m (820ft)	104
19	Avenida Marítima, Playa Blanca	Antigua Escuela, Yaiza	15km (9½ miles)	5hrs	300m (985ft)	120m (395ft)	109
20	Antigua Escuaela, Yaiza	Tasca Mi Garaje, Montaña Blanca	16km (10 miles)	5hrs	480m (1575ft)	390m (1280ft)	113
21	Tasca Mi Garaje, Montaña Blanca	Church, Teguise	14.5km (9 miles)	4hrs30	300m (985ft)	260m (855ft)	118
22	Church, Teguise	Plaza de la Constitución, Haría	14.5km (9 miles)	5hrs	360m (1180ft)	380m (1245ft)	122
23	Plaza de la Constitución, Haría	Harbour, Orzola	12km (7½ miles)	3hrs30	150m (490ft)	430m (1410ft)	127

No	Start	Finish	Distance	Time	Total Ascent	Total Descent	Page
Fuerteventura							
24	El Puertito	El Puertito	12km (7½ miles)	4hrs	200m (655ft)	200m (655ft)	137
25	Gran Valle	Gran Valle	25km (15½ miles)	8hrs	600m (1970ft)	600m (1970ft)	139
26	Ventura Shopping Centre, Playa de Jandía	Ventura Shopping Centre, Playa de Jandía	15.5km (9½ miles)	5hrs30	890m (2920ft)	890m (2920ft)	144
27	Costa Calma	Hotel Meliá Gorriones	12km (7½ miles)	3hrs30	30m (100ft)	30m (100ft)	148
28	Cardón	Cardón	4 or 9.5km (2½ or 6 miles)	1hr30 or 3hrs	150 or 210m (490 or 690ft)	150 or 210m (490 or 690ft)	153
29	Vega de Río Palmas	Ajuy	13km (8 miles)	4hrs	100m (330ft)	350m (1150ft)	155
30	Tiscamanita	Tiscamanita	13km (8 miles)	4hrs	500m (1640ft)	500m (1640ft)	158
31	Calle General Franco, Antigua	Bus stop, Betancuria	6km (3¾ miles)	2hrs	350m (1150ft)	210m (690ft)	162
32	Casillas del Ángel	Casillas del Ángel	14.5km (9 miles)	4hrs30	550m (1805ft)	550m (1805ft)	166
33	Tindaya	Tindaya	17km (10½ miles)	5hrs	530m (1740ft)	530m (1740ft)	170
34	Lajares	El Cotillo	9.5 or 22km (6 or 13½ miles)	3 or 7hrs	100m (330ft)	150m (490ft)	175
35	Football Ground, Lajares	Football Ground, Lajares	10km (6¼ miles)	3hrs15	200m (655ft)	200m (655ft)	179

No	Start	Finish	Distance	Time	Total Ascent	Total Descent	Page
36	El Porís	El Campanario, Corralejo	8km (5 miles)	2hrs30	50m (165ft)	50m (165ft)	181
37	Punta de Jandía	Promenade, Morro Jable	20km (12½ miles)	5hrs	250m (820ft)	250m (820ft)	186
38	Promenade, Morro Jable	FV-2 road, Barranco de Pecenescal	16km (10 miles)	5hrs	400m (1310ft)	350m (1150ft)	191
39	FV-2 road, Barranco de Pecenescal	La Pared	16km (10 miles)	5hrs	270m (885ft)	270m (885ft)	197
40	La Pared	Church, Pájara	24km (15 miles)	8hrs	850m (2790ft)	700m (2295ft)	201
41	Church, Pájara	Bus stop, Betancuria	17km (10½ miles)	5hrs30	710m (2330ft)	520m (1705ft)	207
42	Bus stop, Betancuria	La Cancela, Tefía	18km (11 miles)	6hrs	340m (1115ft)	530m (1740ft)	212
43	La Cancela, Tefía	Church, La Oliva	18km (11 miles)	5hrs30	250m (820ft)	340m (755ft)	217
44	Church, La Oliva	Harbour, Corralejo	25km (15½ miles)	8hrs	255m (835ft)	455m (1490ft)	221
45	El Muelle, Isla de Lobos	El Muelle, Isla de Lobos	11km (6½ miles)	3hrs	250m (820ft)	250m (820ft)	226

APPENDIX B

Topographical glossary

Apart from a few place-names derived from original Guanche words, most names appearing on maps are Spanish. Many words appear frequently and are usually descriptive of landforms or colours. The following list of common words helps to sort out what some of the places on maps or signposts mean.

agua	water	*grande*	big
alto/Alta	high	*guagua*	bus
arenas	sands	*hoya*	valley
arroyo	stream	*ladera*	slope
asomada	promontory	*llano*	plain
bahía	bay	*lomo*	spur/ridge
bajo/Baja	low	*montaña*	mountain
barranco	ravine	*morro*	nose
barranquillo	small ravine	*negro/negra*	black
blanco/Blanca	white	*nieve*	snow
boca	gap	*nuevo/nueva*	new
cabeza	head	*parada*	bus stop
caldera	crater	*paso*	pass
calle	street	*pequeño*	small
camino	path/track	*pico*	peak
cañada	gully	*piedra*	rock
canal	watercourse	*pino/pinar*	pine
carretera	road	*playa*	beach
casa	house	*plaza*	town square
caseta	small house/hut	*presa*	small reservoir
collada/degollada	col/gap/saddle	*puerto*	port
colorada	coloured	*punta*	point
cruz	cross/crossroads	*risco*	cliff
cueva	cave	*roja*	red
cumbre	ridge/crest	*roque*	rock
de/del	of the	*san/santa*	saint (male/
el/la/los/las	the		female)
embalse	reservoir	*sendero*	route/path
era	threshing floor	*valle*	valley
ermita	chapel/shrine	*verde*	green
estacion de guaguas	bus station	*vieja/viejo*	old
fuente	fountain/spring	*volcán*	volcano
gordo	fat/giant		

APPENDIX C
Useful contacts

Travel and transport

Inter-island flights
Binter Canarias
tel 902-391392
www.bintercanarias.com

Canaryfly
tel 902-808065
www.canaryfly.es

Inter-island ferries
Lineas Fred Olsen
tel 902-100107
www.fredolsen.es

Naviera Armas
tel 902-456500
www.naviera-armas.com

Bus services
IntercityBusLanzarote
tel928-811522
intercitybuslanzarote.es

TiadheFuerteventura
tel 928-855726
www.maxoratabus.com

Canary Islands tourism
General tourism
www.turismodecanarias.
com

Eco-tourism
www.ecoturismocanarias.
com

Lanzarote
www.turismolanzarote.
com

Fuerteventura
visitfuerteventura.es

Tourist information offices

Lanzarote
Arrecife
tel 928-813174

Ferryport
tel 928-844690

Airport
tel 928-820704

Playa Blanca
tel 928-518150

San Bartolomé
tel 928-522351

Puerto del Carmen
tel 928-513351

Costa Teguise
tel 928-592542

Fuerteventura
Puerto del Rosario
tel 928-850110

Airport
tel 928-860604

Caleta de Fuste
tel 928-163611

Corralejotel
928-866235

Ferryport
tel 928-537183

Gran Tarajal
tel 928-162723

Costa Calma
tel 928-875079

Morro Jable
tel 928-540776

Island Governments (Cabildos)
Cabildo de Lanzarote
www.cabildodelanzarote.
com

Cabildo de Fuerteventura
www.cabildofuer.es

The Great Outdoors

DIGITAL EDITIONS
30-DAY
FREE TRIAL

- Substantial savings on the newsstand price and print subscriptions
- Instant access wherever you are, even if you are offline
- Back issues at your fingertips

Downloading **The Great Outdoors** to your digital device is easy, just follow the steps below:

1 **Download the App** from the App Store

2 **Open the App**, click on 'subscriptions' and choose an annual subscription

3 **Download** the latest issue and enjoy

The digital edition is also available on

The 30-day free trial is not available on Android or Pocketmags and is only available to new subscribers

  pocketmags.com

LISTING OF CICERONE GUIDES

For full information on
all our guides, books and
eBooks,
visit our website:
www.cicerone.co.uk.

Walking – Trekking – Mountaineering – Climbing – Cycling

Over 40 years, Cicerone have built up an outstanding collection of 300 guides, inspiring all sorts of amazing adventures.

 Every guide comes from extensive exploration and research by our expert authors, all with a passion for their subjects. They are frequently praised, endorsed and used by clubs, instructors and outdoor organisations.

All our titles can now be bought as **e-books** and many as iPad and Kindle files and we will continue to make all our guides available for these and many other devices.

Our website shows any **new information** we've received since a book was published. Please do let us know if you find anything has changed, so that we can pass on the latest details. On our **website** you'll also find some great ideas and lots of information, including sample chapters, contents lists, reviews, articles and a photo gallery.

It's easy to keep in touch with what's going on at Cicerone, by getting our monthly **free e-newsletter**, which is full of offers, competitions, up-to-date information and topical articles. You can subscribe on our home page and also follow us on **Facebook** and **Twitter**, as well as our **blog**.

Cicerone – the very best guides for exploring the world.

CICERONE

2 Police Square Milnthorpe Cumbria LA7 7PY
Tel: 015395 62069 info@cicerone.co.uk
www.cicerone.co.uk